Michael Bhim

Pure Gold

T0262480

Methuen Drama

Published by Methuen Drama 2007

1 3 5 7 9 10 8 6 4 2

Methuen Drama
A & C Black Publishers Limited
38 Soho Square
London W1D 3QZ
www.acblack.com

ISBN: 978 1 408 10389 0

A CIP catalogue record for this book
is available from the British Library

Typeset by Country Setting, Kingsdown, Kent

Soho Theatre and Talawa Theatre Company present

Pure Gold
by Michael Bhim

First performed at Soho Theatre on 27 September 2007

Soho Theatre is supported by

  Harold Hyam Wingate Foundation

Performances in the Lorenz Auditorium
Registered Charity No: 267234

Soho Theatre and Talawa Theatre Company
present

Pure Gold by Michael Bhim

Anthony	**Louis Ekoku**
George	**Leonard Fenton**
Samuel	**Dermot Kerrigan**
Paul	**Mark Monero**
Marsha	**Golda Rosheuvel**
Simon	**Clarence Smith**

Director	**Indhu Rubasingham**
Designer	**Mike Britton**
Production Manager	**Matt Noddings**
Lighting Designer	**Oliver Fenwick**
Sound Designer	**John Leonard**
Stage Manager	**Dani Youngman**
Deputy Stage Manager	**Joanne Grabham**
Assistant Director	**Rachel Briscoe**
Wardrobe Supervisor	**Anna Barcock**
Fight Director	**Bret Yount**
Casting	**Nadine Hoare**

Press Representation	**Nancy Poole (020 7478 0142)**

Soho Theatre	21 Dean Street, London W1D 3NE
Admin:	020 7287 5060
Fax:	020 7287 5061
Box Office:	0870 429 6883
	www.sohotheatre.com

Writer

Michael Bhim

Michael Bhim graduated from the Royal Court Theatre Advanced Playwrights course in July 2004 and since, has had his short play, *Night Moves*, performed at the Pleasance Theatre, and various readings of work in progress at Soho Theatre and the Royal Court. In November 2005, he won the Alfred Fagon Award for the play *Daydreams of Hailey*, and in May 2006 was selected to take part in a year-long attachment with Paines Plough Theatre Company called *Future Perfect*. His last production, *Distant Violence* at the Tricycle Theatre, was aimed at raising awareness for the current plight in Darfur. He is currently on attachment at Soho Theatre.

Cast

Louis Ekoku Anthony

Louis Ekoku is 12 years old and trains at Songtime Theatre Arts in Epsom. He has been performing from a very young age with appearances in *Copacabana, Bugsy Malone, Seussical, Oliver!* and recently in the highly successful youth tour of *High School Musical* at Wimbledon Theatre and Epsom Playhouse for Songtime Theatre Arts. He made his West End debut last Christmas in the Olivier Award winning musical *Caroline or Change* at the National Theatre.

Leonard Fenton George

Leonard Fenton trained at the Webber-Douglas School. His first years in the theatre were spent in repertory companies, where he appeared in plays by Harold Pinter and by Samuel Beckett. There, he met John Calder, publisher of Beckett's prose works and has given public readings from these ever since the mid 1960's.

Later theatre includes work at the Royal National Theatre in plays by Turgenev, Moliere, John Arden and Shakespeare; for the Royal Shakespeare Company in plays by Boucicault, Bernard Shaw and Shakespeare; and at the Royal Court in plays by Arden, Howard Brenton and with Billie Whitelaw in *Happy Days*, written and directed by Samuel Beckett.

He played the part of Bardolph to Orson Welles' Falstaff in *Chimes at Midnight*, as Falstaff himself on a tour of *Henry IV*, in the West End productions of *The Seagull* and *The Bed Before Yesterday*, and in Jonathan Miller's *A Midsummer Night's Dream* at the Almeida Theatre. His most recent theatre includes Arthur Miller's *The Price*, an award-winning play at the Menier Chocolate Factory, and a one-man show featuring the writings of Samuel Beckett and songs of Franz Schubert.

Leonard's many television appearances include *Shine on Harvey Moon*, and his long-standing role of Dr Legg in *Eastenders*. He has many film credits to his name, most recently *The Bridge* with Andrea Corr.

Dermot Kerrigan Samuel

Theatre includes *The Life Of Galileo, Paul, Cyrano De Bergerac* (National Theatre), *A Whistle In The Dark, Therese Raquin* (Citizens Theatre, Glasgow), *Serjeant Musgrave's Dance, Troilus And Cressida* (Oxford Stage Company), *This Lime Tree Bower* (Belgrade Theatre, Coventry/Assembly Rooms, Edinburgh), *Dealer's Choice* (Clwyd Theatr Cymru), *Light* (Theatre de Complicité), *The King Of Prussia* (Minerva Theatre, Chichester) *The Imposter, Donny Boy* (Theatre Royal, Plymouth), *The Herbal Bed* (RSC tour), *My Boy Jack* (Hampstead Theatre), *Power Of Darkness, Inheritors* (Orange Tree), *The Phoenician Women, Romeo And Juliet, The Taming Of The Shrew, Woyzeck* (RSC), *Blasted, The Kitchen* (Royal Court), *Richard II* (Royal Exchange, Manchester) and *Trilby And Svengali* (Shared Experience).

Television includes *Sex, Chips & Rock'n'Roll, Persuasion, Romeo And Juliet* and *The Bill*. Film includes *Waking Ned* and *The Innocent Sleep*. Radio includes *Black Train*.

Mark Monero Paul

Theatre includes *The Christ of Coldharbour Lane* (Soho Theatre), *Sing Yer Heart Out For The Lads* (Pilot Theatre Company), *The Country Wife* (Watford Palace Theatre), *Animal* (Soho Theatre and tour), *Adrenalin Heart* (Bush Theatre), *Abyssinia* (Southwark Playhouse), *Pepper Soup* (Lyric Theatre, Hammersmith), *Talking About Men* (Green Room, Manchester, Oval Playhouse), *Local Boy* (Hampstead Theatre), *Invisible Man* (Kings Head), *Warriors in Wasteland* (New End Theatre) and *A Taste of Honey* (Liverpool Playhouse).

Television includes *Skins, Trial and Retribution, Doctors, Waking the Dead, Murphy's Law, Judge John Deed, Casualty, Gimme Gimme Gimme, The Bill, Eastenders, Paradise Club, A Wanted Man* and *The Firm*.

Film includes *Wilt, Sid and Nancy* and *Babylon*.

Golda Rosheuvel Marsha

Film and television includes *Torchwood, The Bill, Coma Girl, Lava, Jesus Christ Superstar* and *Heart and Soul*.

Theatre includes *Angels in America* (Headlong Theatre), *Antony and Cleopatra, Julius Caesar, The Tempest* (RSC), *Hair* (Gate Theatre; National tour), *Release the Beat* (Arcola Theatre), *The Exception and the Rule, The Skin of our Teeth* (Young Vic), *A... My Name is Alice* (Bridewell Theatre; also Assistant Director), *Songs for a New World, Hello Again* (Bridewell Theatre), *We Will Rock You* (Dominion Theatre), *South Pacific* (National Theatre), *Fame* (National tour), *Jesus Christ Superstar* (Lyceum Theatre / National tour), *Tommy* (Shaftesbury Theatre), *Carmen Jones* (Old Vic / European tour), *Extreme Measures, Spring Loaded* (The Place) and *Baby on Board* (Stephen Joseph Theatre).

Concert/cabaret includes *The Cabaret Hour* (Jermyn Street), *The Sun Jet Lounge* (Water Rats), *A Time to Start Living* (Queen Theatre) and *Ruby Turner National Tour* (UK tour).

Clarence Smith Simon

Theatre includes *Shrieks of Laughter* (Soho Theatre), *A Winter's Tale, Pericles, King Lear, Don Juan* (RSC), *The Jamaican Airman Foresees His Death, Our Country's Good, Charity Event* (Royal Court), *The Storm* (Almeida), *The Honest Whore, The Merchant of Venice* (The Globe), *Design for Living, Les Blancs* (Royal Exchange), *Macbeth* (Arcola Theatre), *As You Like It* (Tokyo Globe), *King Lear, Chasing the Moment* (Southwark Playhouse), *Love at a Loss* (Wild Iris Theatre), *Romeo and Juliet, Fuente Ovejuna, Yerma, Blood Brothers, Hiawatha* (Bristol Old Vic), *Romeo and Juliet* (Gazebo), *Success or Failure* (Umoja), *All You Deserve* (Temba) and *Smith* (Salzburg National Theatre).

Televsion includes *Doctors, The Last Detective, Holby City, The Eustace Brothers, Waking the Dead, Eastenders, Under Cover Cops, Daylight Robbery, Melissa, Sharman, A Midsummer Night's Dream, Loved Up, Medics, The Bill, Fullstretch, Casualty* and *Ebony*.

Film includes *Mexican Standoff, Star Wars, The Dinner, What My Mother Told Me, Half Moon Street* and *Ford on Waters*.

As a writer/director, Clarence's credits include *The Remnant* and *Johnny Was A Good Man* for Double Edge Theatre. As a director/co-producer, his credits include *Ragamuffin* for Double Edge Theatre and *Some Kind of Hero* for Not the RSC.

Company

Indhu Rubasingham
Director

Theatre includes *Fabulation* by Lynn Nottage and *Starstruck* by Roy Williams (Tricycle Theatre), *Sugar Mummies* by Tanika Gupta (Royal Court Jerwood Theatre Downstairs), *Anna in the Tropics* by Nilo Cruz, *Yellowman* (Hampstead Theatre), *The Morris* by Helen Blakeman, *Yellowman* by Dael Orlandersmith (Liverpool Everyman), *Romeo and Juliet* (Chichester Festival Theatre), *The Misanthrope* adapted by Martin Crimp, *The Secret Rapture* by David Hare (The Minerva, Chichester), *Clubland* and *Lift Off* by Roy Williams, *The Crutch* by Ruwanthie De Chikera (Royal Court Jerwood Theatre Upstairs), *The Waiting Room* by Tanika Gupta, *The Ramayana* adapted by Peter Oswald (National Theatre), *The Ramayana, Time of Fire* by Charles Mulekwa, *Kaahini* by Maya Chowdry (Birmingham Repertory), *A River Sutra* (Three Mill Island Studios), *Shakuntala* adapted by Peter Oswald, *Sugar Dollies* by Klaus Chatten (Gate), *The No Boys' Cricket Club* by Roy Williams, *Party Girls* by Debbie Plentie, *D'yer Eat With Yer Fingers?!* and *D'yer Eat With Yer Fingers?! – The Remix* (Theatre Royal Stratford East), *A Doll's House* (Young Vic Studio), Associate Director on *Bombay Dreams* and *Rhinoceros* (UC Davis, California). Indhu has most recently directed *Heartbreak House* by G.B. Shaw at Watford Palace Theatre.

Opera includes *Another America* by Errollyn Wallen (Sadler's Wells).

Mike Britton Designer

Recent design work includes *Henry V* (Royal Exchange Manchester), *Glass Eels* (Hampstead Theatre), *Noises Off* (Liverpool Playhouse), *Nakamitsu* (The Gate), *That Face* (Royal Court), *Don't Look Now* (Sheffield Lyceum and Lyric Hammersmith), *The Winter's Tale, Pericles* (RSC Swan), *Coriolanus, Antony and Cleopatra* (Shakespeare's Globe), *Mirandolina* (Royal Exchange Manchester), *Period of Adjustment* (Almeida), *Walk Hard* (Tricycle), *Comfort Me With Apples* (Hampstead and tour), *Twelfth Night* (Theatre Royal Plymouth/ Thelma Holt Productions), *The Morris* (Everyman Theatre Liverpool), *The Comedy of Errors, Bird Calls* (Sheffield Crucible), *Doctor Faustus* (Liverpool Playhouse), *John Bull's Other Island* (Lyric Belfast), *Tartuffe, The Gentlemen From Olmedo, The Venetian Twins, The Triumph of Love, Dancing at Lughnasa* (Watermill), *The Age of Consent* (Pleasance Edinburgh / Bush Theatre) and *Who's Afraid of Virginia Woolf?* (Oxford Playhouse).

Oliver Fenwick
Lighting Designer

Theatre credits include *Kean* (Apollo Theatre, West End), *Glass Eels, Comfort Me With Apples* (Hampstead Theatre), *Restoration* (Bristol Old Vic and Headlong tour), *Henry V, Mirandolina* (Royal Exchange), My Fair Lady (Cameron Mackintosh/National Theatre Tour production), *The Caretaker, Comedy of Errors, Bird Calls, Iphigenia* (Crucible Theatre, Sheffield), *The Doll's House* (West Yorkshire Playhouse), *Sunshine on Leith* (Dundee Rep & Tour), *Heartbreak House* (Watford Palace), *A Model Girl* (Greenwich Theatre), *The Solid Gold Cadillac* (Garrick Theatre, West End), *The Secret Rapture* (Lyric Shaftesbury Avenue), *Noises Off, All My Sons, Dr. Faustus* (Liverpool Playhouse), *On The Piste* (Birmingham Rep), *The Chairs* (Gate Theatre), *Follies, Insignificance* and *Breaking the Code* (Theatre Royal, Northampton), *Tartuffe, The Gentleman From Olmedo, The Venetian Twins, Hobson's Choice, Dancing at Lughnasa, Love in a Maze* (Watermill Theatre), *Fields of Gold, Villette* (Stephen Joseph Theatre),

Cinderella (Bristol Old Vic), *Hysteria* and *Children Of A Lesser God* (Salisbury Playhouse).

Opera credits include *Samson et Delilah, Lohengrin* (Royal Opera House), *The Trojan Trilogy* and *The Nose* (Linbury ROH), *The Gentle Giant* (The Clore ROH), *The Threepenny Opera* (for the Opera Group) and *L'Opera Seria* (Batignano Festival).

John Leonard
Sound Designer

John Leonard started work in theatre sound 35 years ago, during which time he has provided soundtracks for theatre productions and exhibitions all over the world.

Theatre work for Druid: *Leaves; Empress Of India, The Year Of The Hiker & DruidSynge*. Other theatre includes: *In Celebration* (West End); *Kiss Of The Spider Woman* (Donmar & UK Tour); *The Enchantment* (National Theatre); *Blithe Spirit* (Watford Palace Theatre); *Kean* (UK tour and Apollo West End); *Martha, Josie and the Chinese Elvis* (Birmingham Rep); *Donkey's Years, Summer and Smoke* (West End); *Translations* (Princeton and Broadway); *2000 Years, Paul, The UN Inspector, Jumpers* (also West End and Broadway) (National Theatre); *Antony and Cleopatra, Much Ado About Nothing, The Prisoner's Dilemma, Romeo and Juliet* (RSC); *The Old Masters, The Birthday Party* (Birmingham Repertory Theatre and West End); *The Odd Couple, The Entertainer, Still Life, The Astonished Heart, Ma Rainey's Black Bottom, The Anniversary, The Flint Street Nativity* (Liverpool Playhouse); *Becket, Les Liaisons Dangereuses, Sweet Panic, Absolutely! (Perhaps), The Anniversary, Losing Louis, The Master Builder* (also tour), *Private Lives* (also Broadway), *Embers, Smaller* (West End); *Midnight's Children* (London, on tour and New York); *The Mercy Seat, ID, Whistling Psyche, Brighton Rock,*

Macbeth, Hedda Gabler, The Hypochondriac (Almeida); *The Dwarfs, Guantanamo* (also West End) (Tricycle Theatre); *Under Milk Wood, Amazing Grace, A Child's Christmas in Wales, A Christmas Carol* (Wales Theatre Company).

Exhibitions: Madame Tussaud's in London, New York, Amsterdam, Warwick Castle and Shanghai.

Awards: Drama Desk, Sound Designer of the Year.

Bret Yount
Fight Director

Bret Yount trained as an actor at the Guildford School of Acting, and has worked professionally both as an actor and a Fight Director. Bret is currently a member of Equity's Fight Directors Register, a Certified Teacher with the Society of American Fight Directors (SAFD) and a Master Teacher with the British Academy of Stage and Screen Combat (BASSC). Bret's fight direction work has been seen in such places as the Royal Court Theatre, Haymarket Theatre Basingstoke, Liverpool Playhouse, Theatre Royal Stratford East, Theatre-by-the-Lake, Keswick, York Theatre Royal, Mercury Theatre Colchester, Hull Truck Theatre, Theatre Royal Plymouth, UCC Singapore and the Palais des Festival, Cannes. Recent fight screen credits include *Blue Peter* (BBC), *Against All Odds* (BBC Scotland) and working as the Ass't Swordmaster on *TROY* (Warner Bros).

Bret has also worked extensively as a teacher of stage combat and has taught workshops in the UK, US, Singapore and Germany and is currently the Master-of-Combat at the Royal Academy of Dramatic Art (RADA).

● soho theatre

- ● Produces new work
- ● Discovers and nurtures new writers
- ● Targets and develops new audiences

Under Artistic Director Lisa Goldman, Soho Theatre creates and enables daring and original new work that challenges the status quo by igniting the imaginations of writers, artists and audiences. We initiate new conversations with London and the wider world through projects that celebrate creative participation, internationalism and freedom of expression. We nurture a socially and culturally broad audience for theatre and create a buzz around theatre as a living and relevant art form.

'a foundry for new talent... one of the country's leading producers of new writing' Evening Standard

Soho Theatre has a unique Writers' Centre which offers an invaluable resource to emerging theatre writers. We are the nation's only unsolicited script-reading service which reports for free, on over 2,000 plays per year. Through the Verity Bargate Award, the Writers' Attachment Programme, and a host of development programmes and workshops we aim to develop groundbreaking writers and artists to broaden the definition of new theatre writing. Our learning and participation programme Soho Connect includes the innovative Under 11's scheme, the Young Writers' Group (18–25s), Script Slam and an annual site-specific theatre piece with the local community, *Moonwalking in Chinatown*, in September 2007.

Alongside our theatre productions, Soho Theatre presents a high profile late night programme with a mixture of groundbreaking comedy and performance from leading and emergent artists. We also curate a vibrant talks series and other events, encouraging the conversation to spill over into our new and reasonably priced Soho Theatre Bar.

Contemporary, comfortable, air-conditioned and accessible, Soho Theatre is busy from early morning to late at night.

'London's coolest theatre by a mile' Midweek

● soho theatre

21 Dean Street
London W1D 3NE

Admin: 020 7287 5060
Box Office: 0870 429 6883

www.sohotheatre.com

Soho Theatre Bar

The Soho Theatre's late-licence bar is a comfortable and affordable place to meet in central London.

The Terrace Bar

The Terrace Bar on the second floor serves a range of soft and alcoholic drinks.

Email information list

For regular programme updates and offers visit www.sohotheatre.com

Hiring the theatre

Soho Theatre has a range of rooms and spaces for hire. Please contact the theatre on 020 7287 5060 or go to www.sohotheatre.com for further details.

● soho theatre

Staff

Artistic Director: Lisa Goldman
Executive Director: Mark Godfrey

Board of Directors
Nicholas Allott – *chair*
Sue Robertson – *vice chair*
Norma Heyman
Roger Jospé
Michael Naughton
David Pelham
Roger Wingate
Christopher Yu

Honorary Patrons
Bob Hoskins *President*
Peter Brook CBE
Simon Callow
Sir Richard Eyre CBE

Writers' Centre and Soho Connect
Writers' Centre Director:
Nina Steiger
Soho Connect Director:
Suzanne Gorman
Soho Connect Workshop Leader:
Ashmeed Sohoye
Director of Talks:
Stephanie Merritt

Administration
General Manager:
Catherine Thornborrow
Deputy General Manager:
Erin Gavaghan
Casting Director:
Nadine Hoare
*Assistant to Artistic Director &
Executive Director:*
Nicola Edwards
Financial Controller:
Kevin Dunn
Book Keeper:
Elva Tehan

Marketing, Development and Press
Marketing and Development Director:
Elizabeth Duducu/Jacqui Gellman
Development Manager:
Zoe Crick
Marketing Consultancy:
Spark Arts Marketing
Marketing Manager:
Nicki Marsh
Press and Public Relations:
Nancy Poole (020 7478 0142)
*Marketing and Development
Assistant:*
Zebina Nelson-Myrie
Web Administrator:
Will Sherriff-Hammond
Audience Development Officer:
Annabel Wood

Box Office and Front of House
Front of House Manager:
Jennifer Dromey
*Box Office and
Audience Development Manager:*
Steve Lock
Deputy Box Office Manager:
Danielle Baker
Box Office Assistants:
Lou Beere, Philip Elvy, Lynne Forbes,
Lucy Hayton, Eniola Jaiyeoba, Helen
Matthews, Ian Marshall, Leah Read,
Traci Leigh Scarlett, Tom Webb and
Natalie Worrall.
Duty Managers:
Colin Goodwin, Martin Murphy,
Michael Owen and Sandy Rass.
Front of House staff:
Carla Almeida, Beth Aynsley, Max
Fedyk, Gus Gowland, Juliette
Haygarth, Kate Mulley, Monique
Sterling, Gemma Strong, Stephanie
Thomas and Nida Vohra.

Production
Production Manager:
Matt Noddings
Technical Manager:
Nick Blount
Head of Lighting:
Christoph Wagner
Technician:
Natalie Smith

● soho theatre

The Soho Theatre development campaign

Soho Theatre receives core funding from Arts Council England, London. In order to provide as diverse a programme as possible and expand our audience development and outreach work, we rely upon additional support from trusts, foundations, individuals and businesses.

All of our major sponsors share a common commitment to developing new areas of activity and encouraging creative partnerships between business and the arts.

We are immensely grateful for the invaluable support from our sponsors and donors and wish to thank them for their continued commitment. Soho Theatre has a Friends Scheme in support of its education programme and work developing new writers and reaching new audiences. To find out how to become a Friend of Soho Theatre, contact the development department on 020 7478 0109, email development@sohotheatre.com or visit www.sohotheatre.com.

Sponsors:
Angels The Costumiers, Arts & Business, Bloomberg, International Asset Management, Rathbones, TEQUILA\ London

Major Supporters and Education Patrons:
Anonymous ● Tony and Rita Gallagher ● Nigel Gee ● Paul Hamlyn Foundation ● Roger Jospé ● Jack and Linda Keenan ● John Lyon's Charity ● The Pemberton Foundation ● Carolyn Ward ● The Harold Hyam Wingate Foundation ●The City Bridge Trust

Soho Business Members:
Goodman Derrick ● ilovesoho.com

Trusts and Foundations:
Anonymous ● The Andor Charitable Trust ● The Sydney & Elizabeth Corob Charity ● The Earmark Trust ● Hyde Park Place Estate Charity ● The Mackintosh Foundation ● The Rose Foundation ● Leopold de Rothschild Charitable Trust ● The Royal Victoria Hall Foundation ● Saddlers' Company ● Teale Charitable Trust ● Bruce Wake Charitable Trust ● The Kobler Trust ● The Carr-Gregory Trust

Dear Friends:
Anonymous ● Jill and Michael Barrington ● David Day ● John Drummond ● Madeleine Hamel ● Michael and Mimi Naughton ● Hannah Pierce ● Nicola Stanhope● Diana Toeman

Good Friends and Friends:
Thank you also to the many Soho Friends we are unable to list here. For a full list of our patrons, please visit www.sohotheatre.com

Registered Charity: 267234

Talawa Theatre Company

Talawa Theatre Company celebrated its twenty-first anniversary in February 2007 and is the UK's foremost Black theatre company. We've produced more than forty plays, including African, Caribbean and British classics alongside exciting new writing. Through our weekly Noticeboard, monthly salons, and annual summer school we contribute to the development of theatre practitioners in all areas of the theatre. We are passionate about making and documenting our contribution to British theatre.

Talawa began as an actors company, producing a stage adaptation of CLR James's seminal work 'Black Jacobins', Shakespeare's King Lear and Anthony and Cleopatra, and Oscar Wilde's 'The Importance of Being Earnest' among others as showcases for Black actors and directors. Now Talawa focuses on developing Black British voices, nurturing talent and welcoming new audiences.

Our weekly Noticeboard is a news outlet for the Black Arts world, providing up-to-date information on a broad range of events, from Black-led theatre to experimental music and art. The monthly Salon, *Talk*Theatre, provides a forum in which Black theatre practitioners and audiences alike can discuss the successes and challenges of Black British theatre today. Finally, the annual summer school (Talawa Young People's Theatre) is an ongoing educational project that is entering its thirteenth year. The four week intensive course culminates in a professional production featuring talented young Black actors in Central London.

We are currently led by Artistic Director Patricia Cumper and Executive Director Deborah Sawyerr. Over the years, as more Black work is produced by mainstream theatres and more Black practitioners make successful careers, we have continued to refine our vision and purpose so that today we are proud to focus on Black British work. Our mission statement says: Talawa Theatre Company is Britain's foremost Black led Theatre Company. We give voice to the Black British experience and we nurture, develop and support talent. We cultivate Black audiences and audiences for Black work. In so doing, we enrich British theatre.

We tell the iconic stories of the Black British experience and invest in the development of the practitioners who bring those stories to the stage. We therefore produce predominantly new writing and work with practitioners throughout the UK.

We strive to produce consistently challenging, innovative and entertaining work. We continue to nurture the writers, directors, designers, administrators and marketers of the future. But most of all, we extend to both practitioners and audiences alike the warmth of a Talawa welcome because we are proud that Talawa Theatre Company is a creative space in which artists of all backgrounds are free to tell the stories that enrich the world in which we all must live.

To find out more about us visit our website at www.talawa.com or at www.myspace.com/talawatheatre

Talawa
Theatre Company

Talawa Writers Group

Talawa Theatre Company is cultivating the next generation of Black British writers to enhance British drama.

Talawa Writers Group strengthens the careers of established and emerging playwrights who are passionate about writing Black British drama. The Group, now in its third year, provides a superb opportunity for 8-10 writers to expand their skills, network with key industry leaders and present their work in a showcase of play readings in the spring of each year.

The Talawa Writers Group forms a direct part of the company's mission to nurture, support and develop talent. Talawa believes that there are many exciting Black British stories to be dramatised on stage, television and screen and is engaged in preparing and assisting writers to be best placed to meet that challenge. The company aims to build the infrastructure and people skills to deliver a dynamic industry of Black British storytelling.

To date the programme has hosted some 26 of Britain's most vibrant and exciting Black, Asian and other minority ethnic writers on the scene. These include Dipo Agboluaje, Bola Agbaje, Amman Paul Singh Brar and even Talawa's current Artistic Director, Patricia Cumper.

The programme lasts twelve months and offers targeted advanced writing lectures from persons at institutions such as Royal Court Theatre, Soho Theatre, The Royal National Theatre, BBC, Channel 4 and others. The writers have open discussions with other known writers such as Kwame Kwei-Armah and Roy Williams. They also make a series of West End and other theatre visits so that they experience and engage with large scale theatre movements and events. Writers meet on 1st and 3rd Wednesdays of every month.

Michael Bhim was a member of Talawa Writers Group in 2006. He presented a piece called 'In Freefall' for the showcase series of readings at Soho Theatre in February 2007 (Unzipped.)

In the past the Group has been funded by Channel 4, Peggy Ramsay, London ITV and now by the BBC. Funding from such major bodies is perhaps the greatest acknowledgement of the importance and success of the group in being an important multicultural resource for expanding British drama.

Pure Gold

Characters

Simon
Marsha
Anthony
Paul
Samuel
George

Acknowledgements

I would like to thank the Peggy Ramsay Foundation for their financial support during the writing of this play. I would also like to thank Clint Dyer, Francis Poet, Dr Harry Derbyshire, Jessica Cooper, Graham Whybrow, Cherry Smyth (for opening my eyes to poetry), Dawn Walton, Hazel McConnell, Femi Elufowoju Jr (Tiata Fahodzi, for giving the play its first hearing.) Pat Cumper (Talawa), Lisa Goldman, and of course Indhu Rubasingham and Nina Stieger, for the incredible love and support, and for being my dramaturgical saviours.

I'd like to dedicate this play to my mother Chandra, and my father George, and sister Jacqueline Michelle, who put up with my mad daily rants – well, mostly by ignoring them. I would also like to thank Elafi who bore witness to the birth of the play's idea over a morning coffee in Greenwich.

Act One

Scene One

Marsha *stands in the kitchen area of a modestly decorated council flat. She is soaking dirty dishes in the sink. Next to the sink is a gas cooker. There are two windows in the flat, one above the sink, the other further downstage left, where* **Simon** *is propped up, looking out down onto the street. He has a large coat and underneath that a crumpled suit, both strung on him loosely. He is mildly drunk. It is four o'clock in the afternoon, and a natural light is pouring through the windows. There is a table in the middle of the room, and stage right is the living area, where a sofa rests in front of a TV. Other than that, there is an indoor clothes rail with clothes on it.*

Simon (*looking down onto the street in awe*)　You see that? Look how elegant the roof comes down on that car, huh? . . . Electronic perfection, as perfect as nature . . . I mean, you ever seen something so beautiful?

Marsha　I don't care about a stupid car, Simon.

Simon　Stupid? (*Turning to her.*) You know, baby, ignorance is so unattractive. (*Looking back outside.*) . . . How can you even say that?

Marsha　It is, it's stupid, you're being stupid, you're four hours late, you stink!

Simon (*turning to her*)　God, and you got any other compliments today? Why you gotta be so insulting? (*He smells himself.*) And I don't smell.

Marsha (*to herself*)　Why do I bother? (*She goes to the indoor washing line and begins folding the clothes into a pile.*)

Simon (*considering the word*)　. . . Stupid . . . Honestly, Marsh. (*Slight pause.*) If I had a car like that, no lie, I'd be having such a good time, I swear I'd feel like I was on a date with Halle Berry.

Marsha　Is that supposed to be funny?

Simon　No. (*Slight pause.*) I mean, Marsh . . . (*Pause.*) Look up for a sec . . . just a sec.

Marsha (*reluctantly stops what she's doing and looks up at him*) What?

Simon　Now hear what I'm gotta tell you. (*Painting the picture.*) You sit down inside it, right, like I did, Paul sitting next to me . . . Me, my hand on the gearstick . . . The firm leather steering wheel . . . And it's like, you lift your foot off the clutch, and there it is, you can feel the gas, you can feel how thirsty she is, and boom! She pulls away. She takes off before you even expect it. And I can get me one of these things, hon, if . . . (*Noticing* **Marsha**.) Come on, babe, crunch your face up any more and I'll have to tell everybody I'm married to a raisin.

She stares at him, unimpressed, and continues folding the clothes.

What now?

Marsha (*stopping again*)　You were supposed to have an interview today.

Simon　I did.

Marsha　But instead you're driving around the high street with a forty-five-year-old that thinks he's the next Batman, and you –

Simon　What about me?

Marsha　Well, where else apart from Deptford, Simon, would you find grown men who'd want to emulate cartoon characters? Showing off, proud for nothing, whizzing around the streets like two clowns in a teacup. (*Slight pause.*) Here! (*She throws a pair of tights at him.*)

Simon　What's . . . ?

He catches tights, realises what it is. He holds it up; it unravels.

You're giving me tights?

Marsha　Yeah, go play superhero! You and that big-headed idiot . . . Go on, get out of here . . .

She heads off into the bedroom holding an armful of clothes.

Simon (*finding her amusing, left standing by himself*)   Oh Marsh . . .

He follows her. He stands outside the bedroom, leaning against the door frame.

Simon   Hey, come on now. (*Slight pause.*) I wouldn't exactly say that your mother makes me feel comfortable to wanna stay round her house now, do I? But you don't hear me insulting your family's attributes, do you? He's my cousin, for God's sake.

Marsha *doesn't reply.*

Simon   I mean, you don't like the shape of his head, fair enough, but that's success you're seeing outside. And there ain't nothing wrong with a man being proud of what he's got. Animals do it, don't they? You see the way peacocks carry on these days, feathers all out and shit? . . . Don't even feel like going zoo, the way they keep showing off and trying to outshine you all the time. (*Pause.*) Why you gotta insult him about his head, anyway?

Marsha (*entering from bedroom and pushing past him*)   Simon, if someone's big-headed it does not have to be taken literally all the time.

Simon   So what are you saying then?

Marsha   He's egotistical, and I find it disgusting.

Simon   He's a good guy . . . And anyway I needed the company.

Marsha   And what am I?

Simon   Well, see . . . I needed male company, baby . . . I needed to clear my head, that's all.

Marsha (*sarcastically*)   Of course, a whole day of head-clearing for Simon, why deprive him.

Simon (*feeling insulted*)   You know, that sarcasm, it's just damn annoying! My heads spinning as it is!

Marsha   Well, what d'you expect? You're drunk!

Simon (*straightening himself up*)   I'm . . . (*With clumsy composure.*) I had a drink, OK, woman? (*Pause.*) I had a drink . . . I am not drunk. (*Simultaneously demonstrating.*) If I were drunk, you think I'd be able to stand up straight – look at me . . . or walk in a straight line? Talking at the same time. Which drunk man can do this? Touch his nose, close his eyes, spin – (*He clatters into a chair and stumbles over.*)

Marsha (*irate*)   Get up and stop making a fool out of yourself!

Pause.

Simon (*lying in the floor*)   I think I got a headache . . .

Long pause.

Marsha   I want to know how it went.

Simon (*getting up*)   What?

Marsha   The interview?

Simon (*straightening himself up*)   What interview?

Marsha   What d'you mean, 'What interview?'

Simon (*brushing himself off*)   Oh, you mean that? . . . Yeah, perfect.

Marsha   It was perfect? In what way?

Simon (*sarcastic*)   Well, MI6 girl, they liked me so much they ordered a helicopter and flew me out to City Airport to have lunch.

Marsha (*playing along*)   Oh, did they now?

Simon   Yes, they did . . . I figured they wanted to show me how seriously they wanted me.

Marsha   So it was that bad, huh?

Simon   I dunno why I'm wasting my time, I didn't like it, I knew I wouldn't like it. You ever tried to say something, then you start to realise that you don't even know the meaning of what you're sayin' halfway through?

Marsha   Life's about going through things you don't like.

Simon   What are you talking about? Things I don't like? So I'm born to eat shit? (*Slight pause.*) I mean, I had that 295 route since I was twenty-two. And one old woman makes a fuss, suddenly London General drop me just like that, no goodbye, no warning, no thank you for years of service.

Marsha   So take them to the union. Stop moaning. Your friends were willing to support you, weren't they?

Simon   And who's going to take my word over some old Englishwoman?

Marsha   Well, at least go and find out. You have every right to put your side of the argument across . . . instead of staying silent.

Simon   Yeah, maybe I'll do that. I'll think about it.

Marsha   Then if you did that, I bet you'd get your job back in less than a fortnight and I could return to my studying –

Simon   Marsha!

Marsha   What?

Simon   Please.

Marsha   What? I'm just trying to make you see that there's still an opportunity.

Simon   (*going to collect his bag, which is at the door*)   How? Suffocating me with your optimism?

Marsha   (*beginning to wash the dishes*)   Optimism creates luck, and that's what you need a lot of right now.

Simon   (*turning to her in disgust*)   Luck?

Marsha   Yes, luck.

Simon   This morning, before the interview, I couldn't get out of bed, like I was a Flake, stuck in its wrapper, wrapped up on the bed. You know why?

Marsha   No, tell me, why were you like a Flake?

Simon   Cos all you been talking about is luck all the time. (*Slight pause.*) I mean, I couldn't get out of bed. And I'm working it out, you know, left side or right. If I get out of bed on the left side, it might somehow make the bus late, you know? (*Slight pause.*) After about twenty minutes, I'm just staring at the ceiling and all the grey walls around me like as if I'm in some enlarged coffin. I didn't know what was lucky or unlucky or what. I just lay there. As if luck would just shine down on me once. Once! I'd be happy.

Marsha   Well, it would if you let it.

Simon   See, there you go with all this optimism again.

Marsha   It's not optimism.

Simon   It is. (*Dumping his bag on the table.*)

Marsha   Simon, please.

Simon   What?

Marsha   Please, not on the table.

Simon   It's just a bag!

Marsha   Yes, and I don't want it on the table! It's probably been dragged –

Simon (*interrupting*)   All right, all right.

When she turns, he mimics her when putting his bag on the floor.

Marsha (*without turning around*)   I can see what you're doing.

Simon   What am I doing?

Marsha *gives him a look, and instantly he breaks into a smile.*

Simon (*with gesture*)   . . . What? (*Pause.*) How you always seem to know exactly what I'm doing? Creeping me out.

Marsha   Well, we can't have the blind leading the blind, can we?

Simon   Women, I tell you, I figured it out . . . bunch of supernatural witches. Suck you in with their beauty, and make you think that life's sweet, until you realise it's a trap. If you don't say the right things you're in trouble. You stay out late without saying where you're going, you're in trouble. You even buy her something nice for no reason, just to say you love her . . . She'll think you're up to something, trying to hide some shit, and – guess what? . . . You're still in trouble.

He stands looking at her.

Marsha (*turning round, noticing him*)   Why don't you sit down? You look restless.

Pause. He continues standing.

Simon   You still care about me?

Marsha   What kinda question's that?

Simon   I'm asking you a question.

Marsha   You never seem remotely interested whether I care about you or not.

Simon *remains silent.*

Marsha (*drying her hands on her hips*)   OK, I do. Of course I do, you dope.

She walks up to him.

Simon   Why you so content?

Marsha   Well, why wouldn't I be, Si?

Simon   Because there's all these things you're not doing and we're not doing.

Marsha   Yes, but we're here together, aren't we?

Simon   And that's enough, huh? To be together?

Marsha   Yes.

Simon   . . . That's such a working-class way of looking at things. It's almost painful to hear that.

Marsha (*laughing*)   Shush, there's no such thing. (*She pinches his side.*)

Simon   Ow! Hey, stop that! . . . It's just – like I said to you once before, you gotta see our family like a ship.

Marsha (*looking admiringly at him, not really listening; playfully*) Oh, a ship, is it?

Simon (*passionately*)   And the ship needs a captain, and I believe I'm steering that ship. I'm the captain, you understand?

Marsha (*still not listening; on the verge of laughter*)   Oh, you're the captain? Of course. And you're a good captain.

Simon   And there's gotta be an element of trust in the decisions I'm making, which I feel will bring us prosperity.

Marsha (*not listening; almost dreamily*)   You know, you look beautiful in a shirt and tie.

Simon (*outraged*)   Ain't you listening to me?

Marsha   I'm listening!

Simon (*somewhat fed up; putting her hands down*)   Come on, your hand are wet.

Marsha   Well, I've been washing up, hon . . . If you try it once in a while you'll find out that it's perfectly normal to have wet hands.

Pause. **Simon** *eventually sits down.* **Marsha** *stands looking at him for a while, then returns to wash the dishes. Long pause.*

Simon (*in a huff*)   Where's Anthony?

Marsha   He should be home soon.

Simon   Let me take a fiver off you to give to him.

Marsha   I can't, I don't get paid till next week.

Simon   I'll give it back to you.

Marsha   I don't have it!

Simon   But you must have, the amount of change I always see lying around. I saw ten pound just lying on the bedside table this morning.

Marsha   Yes, and I need that for buying milk and things, not to have you throwing money at him when he wants it.

Simon   Who's throwing money? My son wanted a new pair of trainers the other day.

Marsha   So what if he does?

Simon   He's at a new school. He's got to fit in. You think I want him having no confidence?

Marsha   You gain confidence by what you know in your mind, not by what you wear.

Simon   Yeah, great, have a great mind but look like a tramp? Let's see how far he gets.

Marsha   I'm sorry, but no.

Pause.

And you telling him that he's gotta have this and that to be someone while you're pretending and acting up yourself.

Simon   What the hell you talking about?

Marsha   Telling him you're working when you're not.

Simon   Oh please.

Marsha   Do you know, at school he was asked to write a story about his family, he came and he asked me questions, 'What's Dad doing now? . . . Is he still working? . . . Why doesn't he get up and go to work in the mornings any more?' . . . All the time.

Simon   Well, look how young he is, he's always gonna be asking questions. (*Pause.*) . . . Come on, I mean . . . As a kid didn't he used to love it, when his dad used to drive a bus, Marsh?

Marsha   I know.

Simon   I mean, he'd put my hat on his head, didn't he? I'd pick him up and the smile on his face . . . It was easy to please him, so why change anything? (*Slight pause.*) And it's his birthday soon, he wants me to get him a piano.

Marsha   A what?

Simon   Exactly . . . And where the hell did he even get it into his head to want something so big-looking?

Marsha   Why are you thinking about that anyway? Where the hell would it fit? Look around!

Simon (*getting up*)   You know, you're really starting to annoy me!

Marsha   Where are you going now?

Simon (*walking to the door*)   Out!

Marsha   Out where?

Simon   . . . Anywhere . . . Jobcentre. Who knows, I might get some peace sitting around some asylum seekers, or confiding in a brick wall.

He grabs his coat, taking longer than usual to put it on; he looks quite pathetic. Pause. **Marsha** *watches him.*

Marsha   Lunch, before you go?

Simon (*putting his coat on*)   I ain't hungry, don't worry about me.

Marsha   Si. (*Slight pause.*) Simon.

Simon (*the door half open*)   What?

Marsha   Eat something.

Simon (*without turning back*)   . . . What's the point?

Marsha   . . . I won't say a word. (*Slight pause.*) I'll just make you some lunch. OK?

Pause.

Simon   On condition you stop irritating me.

Marsha   OK, done.

Simon   Fine.

Marsha   Fine.

After a pause, he shuts the door.

Simon   What do we have?

Marsha   Well, what do you want?

Simon   I dunno. Outta the things we got, what do we have, so I can choose somethin'?

Marsha   You want some egg on toast?

Simon   That's all we got?

Marsha   That's all we got, hon. (*Pause.*) I'll make you some egg on toast.

Simon   We don't have no pasta or something?

Marsha   No.

Simon   How about a little mince?

Marsha   No, we don't have that, I said that already.

Simon   All day, egg. Egg and beans, egg and chips, egg and everything. Those farmers out in the country must be billionaires right now cos they've realised that there's a bunch of people in London who can't go a single day without filling their mouths with egg of some kind.

Marsha   You want the egg or not?

Simon (*looking at her begrudgingly*)   . . . I'll have it.

Marsha (*pausing*)   OK. good, we've made some progress.

A silent scene, during which there is a subtle lighting change. **Marsha** *takes out a frying pan from the cupboard and some eggs from the fridge. She begins preparing lunch. Meanwhile* **Simon** *pulls out some papers from his bag, and spreads them out on the table. He turns and observes her. We should watch them for a few minutes.*

Simon   You know what Paul was saying today?

Marsha   No, and I'm not interested.

Simon   He told me, he says it's up to you . . . He said that life's a river, and you can choose to swim it upstream, fighting the current, or have an easy swim downstream just avoiding the rocks.

Marsha   Well, whatever he's implying you shouldn't be listening to him.

Simon   Why not?

Marsha   Because I think he's an idiot, he's always up to something . . .

Simon   You don't know that. Cos see, hon, after what happened today, I'm starting to think what he said, it's true.

Marsha   What happened?

Simon   Well, at the interview right . . . (*Slight pause.*) I was asked to show evidence of a work permit.

Marsha   A permit? What for?

Simon   They didn't believe I was English, did they?

Marsha *starts laughing.*

Simon   You see. You think it's funny?

Marsha   It probably didn't mean anything. Some people make mistakes like that.

Simon   Yeah, why? Ain't I English-lookin' enough? How can you make a mistake like that?

Marsha   Well, am I English-looking?

Simon (*he studies her*)   Yeah, you are . . . You wear some of the fruitiest-looking clothes I've ever seen in my life, and the way you talk, my God, you couldn't be anything else. Whereas me . . . see a face like mine, round black face, applying for a shitty job and suddenly, I'm from Rwanda.

Marsha   Oh, shut up!

Simon   I'm just like that man in *Hotel Rwanda*.

Marsha   The man in that film is American.

Simon   He's Rwandan. You seen his face? See how black he looks?

Marsha   That's Don Cheadle.

Simon   That is not Don Cheadle, I know Don Cheadle. I'm a big fan of Don Cheadle.

Marsha   Well, what d'you want me to tell you, that things like that don't happen?

Simon   I don't care that it happens! Let it happen to the whole lot of immigrants waiting to enter the county, not me! (*Slight pause.*) I mean, I gotta good mind to just go work with Paul.

Marsha   Doing what?

Simon   Whatever's available. He's got that minicab business. ain't he?

Marsha   You haven't even heard if you've got the job yet or not!

Simon   Well, I didn't stay for the interview.

Marsha   You didn't stay? Why not? You told me you went.

Simon   For what? To sit down and have someone look at me in a way that makes me sick in my stomach, like I can't relax in my own country? Forget that! (*Slight pause.*) I worked it out already, if Paul wants to offer me a job pushing around a minicab I can't say no. And I reckon with that I could cover a four hundred deficit each month, clear up those rent arrears doing fuckin' peanuts for this guy. (*Holding out a sheet of paper.*) Look here! I worked it out, no less than four hundred and fifty pounds!

Marsha   You're not going to do anything of the sort.

Simon   Yeah, well, I'm sorry but you're just gonna have to open your mind for a change.

Marsha   Open my mind? Oh, give me a break, with a criminal?

Simon   Yes, open your mind . . . I've never gone behind your
back or done things you didn't want me to do, have I? And
anyway, I know how much you wanna quit working in that
stupid supermarket and get back into the social work, and all
that studying, cos, baby, we both know you got a lot of ambition.
That's why I went to him . . .

Marsha   Bullshit, Simon!

Simon   No, listen, we talked and he said he's willing to come
here tonight and talk through the finer details with us. And it's
only minicabbing and maybe some odd job here and there.

Marsha   What odd job?

Simon   I dunno . . . odd jobs.

Marsha   Simon, you've got so much potential to do other
things . . .

Simon   I don't care!

Marsha   . . . So this is how it is with you?

Simon   Yes, that's right, I'm gonna see what he's got to offer.

Marsha   You had this in your head all this time? (*Pause.*)
Well, I'll tell you now, if he comes here, you will not find me
here tonight!

Simon   Christ! Why not? What is wrong with you? (*Slight
pause.*) You don't take a thirsty man to a river and tell him he
can't drink because the water's dirty.

Marsha   If the water's dirty you keep walking to the next
river . . . Instead of filling your life with excuses, you're not
trying hard enough.

Simon   I've tried, I'm always trying, don't treat me like a
fool.

Marsha   You have to keep trying otherwise you won't get
what you want!

Simon (*shouting*)   I can't get what I want! Don't you get it?!

Simultaneously, in a fluster he pushes his chair back and stands by the window. Pause.

Marsha (*holding a plate of food*)   I just made you food.

Simon   I don't want it! (*Pause. He looks out of the window.*) I married a woman who's happy to dream. To sit in the dark and read shitty magazines about other people's lives . . . And when it comes to really living . . . (*Long pause.*) Where's all the people sayin that London's such a great city? I'm standin here, looking out . . . It's like an overripe fruit. You want a better life, you got no choice but to come here into this ghetto, the roads falling apart, they never fix the water pipes . . . And every way you turn, you can feel that noose, turning tighter round your neck, and loan sharks, just waiting, holding their hands open, pumping their filth through the TV, knowing that you're falling straight into their hands cos you can't survive and pay for a house, and a kid, and good things on this shit . . . And just down the road they wanna open up a great big casino, just to mess around with us, and have our last hopes resting on a gamble . . . a bet. (*Pause.*) Them people up there, them people up in the government, they don't care if you're falling. They just make the way clear so you fall deeper and deeper. (*Pause.*) Everything Paul says it right! One day, we'll all be pushed out to all the smallest areas and the smallest houses! (*Turning to* **Marsha**.) And most of my friends I grew up with are so fucked off at being ignored. I can understand why they've all gone with the BNP cos they're the only ones offering something different . . . And they come to me and they say, it's time to get tough cos no one else's listening! But what about me? Cos if I'm English, if I'm born here, I have every right to live out my ambitions. I want that chance, I want it! Instead of being the dog, instead of working to try put scraps of shit in my gut. We work so hard, backs get bent like rusted iron. And I tell you and you don't give a shit! (*Pause. He looks back outside. Suddenly shouting.*) What happened to you people? What happened?!

Marsha   Please stop that. Stop it!

Simon (*turning back*)   What? You think in that interview if I had said that I was from Greenwich instead of the top end of Lewisham, you think they wouldn't have looked at me a bit different? Thought I was more reliable? . . . It's a curse being born like me in this country, it's a curse!

Marsha   You don't even know what you're saying.

Simon   I know exactly what I'm saying! (*Slight pause.*) Sometimes I wish a big wall of water would just swallow up this place, everything, and just kill off everything. All the buildings, and all the people in it. And when we start again everyone will get a chance to fight over who has what.

Long pause.

Marsha   What do you want from me that I'm not giving you?

Simon   To understand that family are the only people hiring right now.

Marsha   I don't believe that at all, you're just being lazy.

Simon   And what do you know? Your mother's kept you so wrapped up in a cocoon with that fake cosmopolitan bullshit that you don't know nothing about life. Nothing! You're so far up your own arse it's unbelievable!

Marsha   Oh, you're disgusting, you really are.

She heads towards the bedroom to get her coat. **Simon** *follows her and holds her gently.*

Simon   Where are you going?

Marsha (*easing out of his grip*)   We have a son, don't we?

Simon   That's what I'm talking about. Let him come home by himself. Let him be a man!

Marsha   Oh, you mean like you? (*She puts her coat on and grabs her keys.*) Are you something to be proud of right now?

Simon   Am I? I'm giving you a chance to quit that bullshit job.

As she walks past he gets up and grabs hold of her.

Look, Marsh –

Marsha Simon, let go.

He tries to hold her again; reluctantly she lets him.

Simon Why do I always feel that I'm being undermined by you? I want you to understand me.

Marsha *eases out of his grip and heads towards the door.*

Marsha I don't want to hear any more.

She exits.

Simon Well, fine! (*Shouting.*) That's fine! Fucking fabulous! You hear me? Let's just live that ideal life that you want! In this cheap house! With the cheap fucking food! Cheap everything!

There is a gentle banging on the wall from the next-door neighbour. He turns to the wall.

What? Did I make the walls so thin?

He stops shouting. He wipes his face. As he walks back to the table, he gets tangled into a nearby chair and in complete frustration kicks it to pieces. He stands around, flustered. He walks over to the phone, pulls out a piece of paper and dials the number on it. A few seconds later he puts the phone to his ear. waiting to speak.

Slow fade.

Scene Two

It is later in the evening, 6 p.m. **Simon** *and* **Anthony** *are sitting at the dinner table.* **Marsha** *is in the kitchen area cooking.* **Anthony** *is eleven years old.* **Simon** *stares at him. He runs his hand though* **Anthony**'s *hair, almost inspecting it.*

Simon I think it's time for a haircut.

Anthony No.

Simon   Why not?

Anthony   I don't want you cutting my hair.

Simon   You don't want me cutting your hair?

Anthony   No.

Simon   Why?

Anthony   Cos the last time you did it –

Simon   What happened? You didn't like it? The girls loved you! It was beautiful.

Anthony   No it wasn't, Dad. You zigzagged it.

Simon   I what? . . . Zigzagged?

Anthony   Yeah . . . Have you ever seen what SpongeBob's head looks like? That's exactly what you made me look like.

Simon   What d'you mean? Like what? Show me.

Anthony   It was square at the top with lines running through it. (*He gets up.*) Look, like –

Simon *grabs hold of him.* **Anthony** *squeals.*

Simon (*holding him down playfully*)   Where's my rusty scissors, huh? Marsh, you seen 'em?

Marsha *turns round.* **Simon** *looks back at her. She then turns back round and continues preparing dinner.*

Simon   I'm gonna chop all your hair off, and you're gonna have the worst patchiest head ever!

Anthony   Mum! Help!

Simon   Only last week, you used to want me to shave your head clean till you looked like one of those baby chickens.

Anthony   No I never!

Simon   You'd wet the bed, run around and then want a haircut . . . Now you wanna criticise the best haircutter of the eighties and nineties?

Anthony   Yeah, but it's the twenty-first century.

Simon *lets him go.*

Anthony   You've got no style, Dad. Face it, you're crap. Just look in the mirror.

Simon   Hey, come on now, have some respect.

Anthony   But I've seen the pictures!

Simon *makes a playful attempt to grab him again.* **Anthony** *dodges.*

Simon   Those hairstyles were the deciding factor on your entry into this world, boy. If I hadn't made your mum weak with a slick display of a high-top with some patterns and a lean, right now you'd be nothing!

Anthony (*laughing – a threat*)   You want me to ask her then? I'll ask her.

Simon   Go ask her.

Anthony (*leaning back on his chair*)   Mum, Dad's hairstyles were crap, weren't they?

Marsha (*seriously*)   Anthony, go and change your uniform.

Anthony *stops smiling, and leans back to the table.*

Simon   See, she wouldn't admit it!

Anthony (*getting up*)   I'm gonna go change.

Simon   It's all right, don't go just yet.

Marsha *looks at* **Simon***. He looks back at her. Long pause.* **Anthony** *slowly sits back down.*

Simon   So . . . how's school, any good?

Anthony   Yeah . . . it's all right.

Simon   You're not just saying that to please me? You know what we think about yes-men in this house.

Anthony   No, I like it.

Simon   You sure about that?

Anthony Yes, Dad, I'm not a baby, even though you keep talking to me like one.

Simon All right, all right . . . But you're telling me you like school but you dunno what you like? I mean, a man's gotta know what he likes. I didn't get to where I got in life without knowing what I liked.

Anthony I do!

Simon If you don't know, you're not a man!

Anthony I know what I like, Dad!

Simon OK, what? Tell me.

Anthony I told you already, you should know.

Simon OK, what? I forget.

Anthony OK, I'll ask you a question.

Simon Sure, ask me, I'm ready.

Anthony Rachmaninov, who is he?

Simon Wait a minute . . . Rach-man-inov . . . (*He thinks.*) A tennis player.

Anthony You see, what did I tell you? You don't know. (*He laughs.*)

Simon OK, I'm kidding, a racing-car driver?

Anthony No, you don't know, Dad – give up.

Simon OK, OK, so what?

Anthony I'll give you another one.

Simon Shoot!

Anthony Gershwin?

Simon That's an easy one, Gershwin. I told you about Gershwin.

Anthony Then name a song.

Simon   I don't remember the name of a song, but I know who it is.

Anthony   Dad, you don't know.

Simon   Of course I do.

Anthony   I'm talking about the piano!

Simon   OK, it's the piano. But son, you know there's a hell of a lot more to life than making little noises with your fingers!

Anthony   I know, but I like it.

Simon   Yes, I know, but is that all you're learning in school? We send you all the way to a good school.

Anthony   I don't care what school I go to, Dad . . . (*Slight pause.*) You still gonna get me one for my birthday?

Simon   Well, you sure that's what you want?

Anthony   It is. It's definitely what I want!

Simon   I mean, ain't you thought of learning something like, I dunno, something smaller?

Anthony   Like what?

Simon   We'll, well, there's loadsa things – drums, no forget drums. What's that little wooden flute thing?

Anthony   Dad, who plays a recorder? . . . I'm only asking because Mr Wordsworth thinks that I've got natural ability . . . He said if I had a piano to practise on every day, I'll be good enough to join next year's jazz ensemble.

Simon   Mr Wordsworth . . . who's that? Your teacher?

Anthony   Yeah, and after class he asked me to perform a jazz song called 'Misty' in front of everyone, two-handed.

Simon   And you did it?

Anthony   Yeah.

Simon   Hmm . . . Jazz (*To* **Marsha** *proudly.*) You hear that, Marsh? Mr Wordsworth says this boy's got natural ability.

Marsha   Anthony, you've had enough now . . . Are you going to change your uniform or would you prefer me to get mad, which one?

Simon (*to* **Marsha**)   He'll go in a minute. (*To* **Anthony**.) So, you really want this piano?

Anthony   I do, Dad.

Simon (*after a pause*)   Well, look, you tell Mr Wordsworth, right, the only reason why I ain't got you a piano as yet is cos I'm not just gonna buy any old thing.

Anthony   You're gonna get it, yeah?

Marsha   Simon!

Simon   What?

Marsha   Give the child a break.

Simon (*casually*)   We're talking about his birthday. (*To* **Anthony**.) Aren't we?

Anthony   Please, Mum, it's important!

Simon   Exactly, and – you know, I've got an idea.

Anthony   What?

Simon   Maybe I'll get you one of them great big electric pianos. I'm talking massive.

Anthony   Really?

Simon   Can you wait till next week?

Anthony   Yeah.

Simon   Then that's it! It's yours.

Anthony (*celebrating*)   Yes! . . . Can we also get a PlayStation?

Simon   Yeah, I don't see why not!

Anthony   Yeah? You're gonna get all that?

Simon   Of course, easy.

Marsha   Anthony!

Anthony   Yes, Mum?

Marsha   I'm not gonna tell you again, take that bag off the floor, and go change your uniform!

Anthony   Now, Mum?

Marsha   Yes, now – right now!

Anthony *looks at* **Simon**.

Simon (*briefly looking at* **Marsha**)   . . . OK, go on, you'd better do as your mother says.

Anthony *gets up.*

Simon   And when you get back, I wanna hear about this thing with you and the school rugby team.

Anthony   I hate it!

Simon (*calling out to him*)   Why, what d'you have to do?

Anthony (*calling to him from the bedroom door*)   Prop!

Simon   What's a prop do?

Anthony   Nothing, I just have to have someone stick their head between my legs, it's disgusting!

Simon *laughs.* **Anthony** *exits into his bedroom to get changed.* **Marsha** *is packing some food into a plastic container.*

Simon (*looking in* **Anthony**'s *direction*)   My boy . . . Isn't he amazing, huh? Look at him . . . One minute he can't speak, Marsh, and the next . . . he's got his own personality . . . things he likes, things he hates.

Marsha *doesn't respond.*

Simon (*looking at her*)   You know, sometimes . . . (*slight pause*) I'm sure the only reason Napoleon never conquered the whole world is cos he had some woman there in the background messing up all the plans . . . ain't that right, hon? (*Pause.*) . . . And what is it with you? Spending all your time making food for George? That old guy can look after himself – I mean, he owns his own house, and he's a stranger, he's not even family.

Marsha   Simon, I don't appreciate what you're doing.

Simon (*casually*)   . . . I was just having a conversation with the kid.

Marsha   I don't care. Don't fill his head with crazy ideas, he's just a child.

Simon   . . . And it's his birthday soon.

Marsha   And you're misleading him!

Simon   I want him to look forward to something. What's wrong with that?

Marsha   Let's just end this conversation.

Simon   He's the only son I got, but you want me to keep letting him down.

Marsha   I want you to stop lying to him!

Simon   I've practically got a job! I'll have the money.

Marsha   You've got a job? (*She laughs in disbelief.*) Oh, well done, well done.

Simon   That's right. I'm pleased to see you find it so funny.

Marsha   You think you know everything about people, don't you? . . . Your instincts are just so exceptional.

Simon   You're starting to sound like your mother again, you know that?

Marsha (*after a pause*)   You don't know anything about what Paul does. Look at his background – the last time we heard about him he was accused of selling rancid meat to all the shops in the market, do you remember that?

Simon   It's opinions like that, that don't give people a chance in life.

Marsha   Well, who'd want to give him a chance at anything?

Pause. She heads for the door, holding a container of food.

Just for once think about us, and not only yourself.

Simon   . . . Who else am I thinking of, Marsh?

He notices she is no longer paying attention.

Yeah, that's right, go, always, all the time.

He sits at the table, then gets up and starts setting the table. Long pause.

(*Calling out.*) Anthony! . . . Anthony!

Anthony (*entering*)   Yeah, what?

Simon (*holding out three plates*)   Come, take these and put them over on the table.

Anthony *takes the plates and sets the table. Pause.*

Simon   You know your mum don't mean nothing by being so strict about things. (*Pause.*) Sometimes she just gets angry if she thinks you wanna have fun all the time.

Anthony   Yeah, I know. That's what mums are like, innit?

Long pause.

I wrote a story about you at school.

Simon   Really?

Anthony   Yeah.

Simon   What was it about?

Anthony   It was just about how you drive a bus.

Simon   And what did they think?

Anthony   My teacher liked it, I had to read it out in class. Now everyone wants to know how big the engine is.

Simon   Well, bring some of your friends over, I'll tell 'em!

Anthony   . . . Yeah.

Simon   You should!

Anthony   . . . I don't know. Maybe, Dad. I'll think about it.

Simon   Don't worry, you know . . . We'll sort this place out before they come. I've already arranged it. I'll just need you to behave tonight. Don't be making a fuss around Paul!

Anthony   When he comes, can I still hang out with you guys?

Simon   If you behave.

Anthony   Then ask Mum to let me stay here.

Simon   What do you mean, ask her to let you stay? Who said you can't?

Anthony   I have to go stay with Gran tonight, unless you say something.

Simon   Is that so?

Anthony   She said she promised Gran that we'd go and see her before my birthday.

Simon   Well, don't you worry about it. You are staying here. You ain't going nowhere tonight.

Anthony   Tell her, don't forget.

Simon   I'll tell her.

Anthony   Yes! Wicked! I'm gonna drive Uncle Paul's car.

Simon   You like his car that much?

Anthony   You should get something like that, Dad, it'll suit you.

Simon   What, a Porsche? . . . I'll get something ten times better than that.

Anthony   Like what? Ferrari?

Simon   Hey, now that's tempting . . . I might . . . But then again imagine your mother trying to put a whole week's worth of shopping in the back of a Ferrari?

Anthony   Yeah . . . Aston Martin, the DB9?

Simon   How'd you know so much about cars?

Anthony   I read about them.

Simon   Your brain's like a sponge, you know that? (*Slight pause.*) Anyway, how about this, the day you turn seventeen, you get up out of bed and step outside, I'll have a nice brand new MG waiting for you.

Anthony   Really?

Simon   You know what an MG looks like?

Anthony   Yeah. My friend's got one.

Simon   But how can your friend have one, how old is he?

Anthony   He's thirteen. He said his dad's gonna buy him another one next year.

Simon   Yeah, well, dads say a lot of things, so don't take no notice of that.

Anthony   His older brother's eighteen and he's got a Lotus now.

Simon   Yeah, well, maybe when you're eighteen I might get you something much better than a Lotus.

Anthony   But –

Simon (*interrupting*)   Hey, come on, that's enough about it! (*Pause.*) . . . I don't wanna hear about cars or pianos or nothing! . . . Go on, bring the pot here.

They continue setting the table. **Simon** *notices* **Anthony**'s *despondent manner.*

Simon   Come on, son . . .

Anthony *turns round.*

Simon   . . . I'll get you all that stuff . . . All of it. All right? Everything you want, you'll have the best, you'll see.

He runs his hand through **Anthony**'s *hair. They sit down and* **Simon** *dishes some food onto* **Anthony**'s *plate.* **Marsha** *enters. She notices the table is set with the food laid out.* **Simon** *and* **Anthony** *are seated waiting for her to sit down.*

Marsha   Are we sitting at the table today?

Simon   Yep, just like a normal family. It's more civilised.

Marsha *walks over to the table, pulls out a chair and sits down. They begin eating.*

Anthony (*to* **Marsha**)   Mum, where d'you go?

Marsha   Next door.

Simon (*slightly sarcastic*)   That's so caring of you. And how's the lucky man?

Marsha   Fine.

Pause.

Anthony   He must be old. Why does he live by himself?

Simon   He used to live with his wife before she died – she died ten years ago.

Anthony   Is that why he's always drunk, Mum? Cos he's by himself?

Marsha (*to* **Anthony**)   Eat your food!

Pause.

Simon   He asked you a legitimate question.

Marsha *looks at* **Simon** *furiously.*

Marsha (*to* **Anthony**)   I don't ever want to hear you talking about people like that! D'you hear me?

Anthony   I'm sorry.

Simon   Yes, Anthony, no talking about people, because we don't want to judge anybody, OK? Marsha, maybe you should do the same too, huh? When it comes to your opinions of people?

Marsha   Simon, stop antagonising me.

Simon   The kid asks you a question – why can't you just answer the boy? It's ridiculous.

Marsha   Oh please, just shut up for once, you're so full of it.

Simon (*putting his fork down*)   What d'you say? I'm so full of what? (*Pause.*) I mean, you're happier to give our food away to this flipping stranger who's never had to struggle in his life and I'm struggling and you won't let me do my own things.

Marsha   Oh, you're so ignorant, it's unbelievable.

Pause. **Simon** *reaches in his pocket and pulls out a five-pound note.*

Simon   No, see, I just care about my family. (*To* **Anthony**.) Anthony, let me tell you something, boy, you always put your family first. And you know what, I don't have much, but here, put this in your pocket.

He puts the five-pound note on the table in front of **Anthony**.
Anthony *reaches to pick up the money.*

Marsha (*to* **Anthony**)   Leave that alone! (*To* **Simon**.) What are you proving?

Simon (*to* **Anthony**)   Your mother don't like you having nothing, so here.

He reaches in his pocket and pulls out another five-pound note, and slams it on the table in front of **Anthony**.

Simon   Go buy some snacks for yourself in the lunch breaks next week, go buy anything you want. (*Slight pause.*) Go on, put it in your pocket.

Anthony *is unsure whether to take the money, so* **Simon** *picks it up and puts it into* **Anthony**'s *pocket.*

Marsha   Yes, Simon, just keep throwing money at him, show off in front of your son because you're so wealthy.

Simon   Why don't you just shut the fuck up? . . . You're so stupid.

Marsha *throws down her fork.*

Simon   You wanna throw it down harder? Go on . . .

He lifts up **Marsha**'s *plate and throws it down onto the table. The plate breaks.*

Simon   There!

Marsha *stares at him in disbelief.* **Simon** *continues eating.* **Marsha** *gets up and picks up* **Anthony**'s *plate in the middle of him eating, but* **Simon** *stops her.*

Simon   Leave it!

Marsha (*to* **Anthony**, *quietly*)   Go and get ready, we're going to your gran's.

Anthony *gets up.*

Simon (*to* **Anthony**)   Sit back down!

Anthony *sits back down.*

Simon (*to* **Marsha**)   You wanna go Hammersmith tonight, you go by yourself. My boy stays with me.

Marsha (*to* **Anthony**)   Anthony, hurry up!

Anthony *begins moving slowly.* **Simon** *gets up.*

Simon (*to* **Anthony**)   . . . Anthony, do you want to stay here tonight?

Anthony *is hesitant to answer.*

Simon   You wanna hang out with me and Uncle Pauly tonight?

Anthony *looks at* **Marsha**.

Simon   He wants to stay.

Marsha *tries to grab hold of* **Anthony** *but* **Simon** *grabs her and pushes her away. Not realising his strength, he causes her to stumble. She's shocked.*

Simon   Now look what you're doing.

Marsha *exits into the bedroom. She slams the door behind her.* **Simon** *is left holding on to his son. He gets the sense that* **Anthony** *wants to go into the bedroom, so he lets go of him.*

Simon   You better go with your mother.

Anthony *rushes off into the bedroom.* **Simon** *waits for him to shut the door before he rubs his brow in frustration and stares at the bedroom door. He sits back down and puts his head in his hands.*

Scene Three

Some hours have elapsed and **Simon** *is sleeping at the table in the same position as in the previous scene. It is almost midnight. Suddenly the sound of a car pulling up is heard. Simultaneously, the soft reflection of passing headlights illuminate the ceiling and wall of the flat. Two car doors can be heard slamming from a distance. A period of silence, then the intercom buzzes loudly.* **Simon** *jolts up. He gets up and presses the intercom.*

Crackly Voice   Evening, monsieur!

Simon *presses him in, then looks around. He notices the dishes on the table and instantly dumps everything in the sink. He notices food on his shirtsleeve so he takes his shirt off, retrieving a jumper from the bedroom. Suddenly there is a loud banging on the door.*

Simon *opens the door.* **Paul** *is standing behind the door; he wears a thick black leather coat. Under one arm he holds a large brown paper bag. They stare at each other.*

A silence.

Paul   You're naked.

Simon   I'm not naked.

Paul   You shouldn't answer the door to people like that, it suggests other things.

Simon   Well, look. (*Puts his jumper on.*) Not any more now, am I? (*Brightly*) . . . How you doing?

Paul   Me, good, no, I'm great! . . . But what about you? Look at you . . .

Simon   What?

Paul   Your mug.

Simon   What's wrong with it?

Paul   Look like it's been dragged along the fucking staircase.

Simon   I was asleep.

Slight pause. They both look at each other. He smiles.

Paul   . . . Go on, get out the way, gotta let myself in these days, no hospitality.

Simon *moves out of the entrance.* **Paul** *enters the house. Pause.*

Paul   So . . . ?

Simon   Yeah?

Paul   She in?

Simon   Who, Marsh?

Paul   No, your great-grandma, who else?

Simon   No, she's not in.

Paul   The boy?

Simon   No.

Paul   Where they gone?

Simon   . . . Up Hammersmith, stayin' with the mother-in-law.

Paul   Yeah?

Simon   . . . Yeah.

Paul   . . . Maybe you should've told them I was gonna come down tonight. They wouldn't've gone nowhere.

Simon *laughs to himself.*

Simon   Yeah, well, they already had plans.

Paul   Plans are there to be broke. (*Slight pause.*) Ain't that the way?

Simon   Yeah, I suppose . . .

Paul   And they love seeing me, absolutely love it . . . don't they?

Simon   Well, yeah . . .

Paul   What, you think they don't? You think they hate me instead?

Simon   Hate you? No, they love you. Just like you said . . . (*Slight pause.*) I should've told her, really. She was keen on seeing you, so was the boy, talk about you all the time.

Paul   Talk after me, huh?

Simon   Yeah.

Paul   What do they say?

Simon   I dunno . . . this and that . . .

Paul   This and that, huh? . . . Yeah I'll take that . . . this 'n' that.

Slight pause.

Simon   But I'm glad you came!

Paul   I'm glad I'm here! Ecstatic! I get a good feeling every time I come here . . . Like one time I was leaving your flat, getting in my car, and I looked up at your window, and I saw Marsha's face. She was looking down at me, smiling – I think she was smiling. And I felt like she was saying, Paul . . . you're special and the world needs you . . . Gave me a good feeling, you know? . . . Set me off for the rest of the day.

He looks at **Simon.** *Puts his arm around him.*

Paul   You've done well. Proud . . . well proud. You got just the right balance of everything, a good kid, and a wife that's hot enough to never get bored of, you know what I mean? (*He looks around.*) . . . This place is still a fucking dump, though, what you been doing?

Simon   You were here last week, how can I do anything in a week?

Paul   Plus walking up the stairwell, it stinks of piss, I'm about to fucking choke, you know what I mean? Get the council to hose the shit down.

Simon   Yeah, well, I told you, a week is not enough time.

Paul   Did I say the same thing last week?

Simon   You did –

Paul   No I didn't.

Simon   You did, first time you came.

Paul   Well, I must've forgot . . . If I did, well, the way I feel, I just got too many things ticking in my head. Been giving out too much advice but no one's listening.

Simon   It's not about not listening. I just ain't got the money to do nothing yet, hence . . . (*He demonstrates, pointing around the house.*)

Paul   Oh, fuck off! When's that stopped anyone? Beg, borrow, steal if you have to! . . . It's your value system. (*Dumping the bag down on the table.*) You got none . . . Your excuse is about as weak as those black people you see in the paper all the time, complaining about a lack of opportunity 'n' stuff. (*Caribbean accent.*) 'Oh please, people, hear our cries, we're being ignored!' (*He laughs.*) I say fuck you, throw them back in the hole and let them suffer . . . You gotta learn how to hustle . . . I know a decorator.

Simon   He expensive?

Paul   I dunno, his name's Mixer. I'll get him to come round, give you a quote. (*He observes the walls.*) You could do with a re-plastering. (*He starts inspecting the wall. Slight pause.*) Did a spot of plastering up in . . . where was it? (*He thinks.*) Leytonstone, a while back . . . No point now really, Kosovons or Bosnians'll do it, half the price, Poles half the price of that. Had to give up the business, do something else . . . just weren't making nothing. (*Slight pause.*) Came out of Pentonville one time, told the governor, I said, 'Son you better work a bit harder at getting me to do what I do best, cos there's just no work going about. Companies out there are setting the new minimum to one pound fifty, and all them fucking foreigners are loving it. (*Slight pause.*) And I remember, working on the sites before, you know, good money, climbing up roofs and all that, half pissed . . . Blacks, whites, a few of us ex-cons, dropping scaffolds on cars 'n' stuff, all English though, you know, for the most part . . . It was all very harmonious, 'part from the usual – knucklehead, you black cunt, etcetera, etcetera . . . (*Slight pause.*) Didn't bother me . . . Some guys just enjoyed getting beaten up. One of the main reasons I kept going back inside all the time . . . You want a beer?

Simon   Yeah, of course.

Slight pause. **Paul** *gives* **Simon** *a beer. He takes a sip.*

Paul   I used to have the same kind of trouble. Buses, sometimes, passengers, they say some things . . . And I'd just say, fuck it, I'm gonna throw you off the fucking bus, you know what I mean? Don't settle for that kinda thing.

Paul   No, sir. Not at all.

Simon   Cos a man makes his territory, be it a bus, or on a building site, you know what I'm saying . . . You don't take abuse. And if you lose your job over it, then so be it.

Paul   Way of the world, way of the fucking world. Sad to hear about your situation, you loved that job.

Simon   Man, do I look as if I care? I'm happy to be done with it.

Paul   Just how much can you tolerate these days? Or be tolerated?

Simon   Suppose that's the way. That's why we gotta stick together, like family.

Paul   That's right, that's right, make our own opportunities.

Simon   Yes!

Paul   Look out for each other, you know. You have my back, I have yours, an' you know I've got yours.

Samuel *appears at the door.*

Samuel   Knock, knock!

Paul   Where you been?

Samuel   What's it matter? . . . (*Slight pause.*) But it's good to see you're at it again. Black allegiance talk, and all that shite, hear you mouthing off from the fucking staircase . . . Just one thing though, lads. When yous all decide to change the world 'n' all, give us a piece of the action. (*To* **Simon**.) And another thing, serious things, whatever that bastard says about hard work, don't buy into it. Fucking skinny bastard's never done a hard day's work in his life. Never.

Simon   Well, that's your opinion, I think he's all right.

Pause. **Samuel** *stares at* **Simon**, *then at* **Paul**.

Samuel   You would, you don't know him.

Simon   What's that supposed to mean?

Paul (*to* **Simon**, *highly animated*)   Hey, Simmy, come here! . . . Quick introduction, right. OK, Sammy meet Simmy, Simmy, Sam. How's that, huh? You like that? Simmy Sammy, Sammy Simmy, right?

Simon   Yeah, I got it.

Paul   I got a sharp tongue. What can I say?

Samuel   Yeah, you wouldn't wanna guess how it got that way, hey, Paul?

Simon   How?

Samuel   He's got a dick the size of a peanut.

Paul   What the fuck hell you talking about?

Samuel   From the horse's mouth . . . what can I say? Don't drink alcohol around me, pal, get all emotional, can't keep that mouth of yours shut.

A car horn beeps loudly.

Where's the window at?

He spots it and rushes over to the window.

Paul   I've known this guy so fucking long, it's actually unhealthy.

Samuel   You're not sick of me so soon now, are ya, love?

Paul (*to* **Samuel**)   What you think? (*To* **Simon**.) I see him more times than you probably see your wife. Now how miserable is my life, huh? You, you got nothing to complain about, trust me.

Simon   You don't know my wife, mate, typical woman, fusses over any decision I make, puts her head in everything I do.

Paul   Women need to know their place, it's a man's world, and it's the man that makes the decisions.

Samuel   Gentlemen, please.

Paul   Yeah, what?

Samuel   I'm a feminist, so shut the fuck up.

Paul   You a feminist?

He and **Simon** *start laughing.*

Samuel   Yeah, that's right!

Samuel *turns back round and begins making hand signals out of the window. He moves his arms like someone directing a plane to land on a runway.*

Paul   What the hell you doing?

Samuel   Shut your gob for a sec, I'm reading something. (*He finishes making signals.*) Mo's saying . . . hold on . . . can you finish up wanking, cos he's shooting off in five minutes.

Paul   Forget it, tell him to frikkin' wait, he can wait.

Samuel   Hold on . . . (*Still translating.*) . . . He says he's got a date.

Paul   So what? I don't give a shit. We just got here, didn't we?

Samuel   Fair enough, I'll tell him.

He turns back to the window and firmly sticks his two fingers out the window, followed by a signal to suggest he'll cut the person's head off. He then closes the curtain.

All done.

Paul (*looking at his watch*)   We've only been here five minutes, we got plenty time . . .

Simon   Nice watch.

Paul   This? (*He looks at his watch again.*) We met each other in central London. It was singing out to me in a shop window. And I dunno. In a way it kinda makes me feel like I'm Sean Connery.

Samuel   You mean the skinny, ugly, black Sean Connery.

Paul (*staring at* **Samuel**, *irate*)   You trying to be funny? You think that's funny? Who's black and ugly?

Samuel (*after a pause*)   Er . . . maybe your cousin break the news to you gently. (*He smiles.*)

Paul   Irish cunt, you think you're so funny. (*He grabs a beer from the bag and throws it to him.*) Here, cool yourself down.

Samuel *lets the bottle fly past him. It smashes on the floor.*

Samuel   Oh dear, now look what you done.

Paul   Now why the fuck d'you do that for?

Simon   It's all right . . . I'll clean it . . . I do it all the time.

Paul   You do what all the time? Throw fucking bottles around? Smash the place up?

Samuel (*looking in the sink*)   Actually, I think he does. (*He picks up a broken plate from the sink.*)

Simon   I'll clean it. I'll clean it. Seriously, relax. It's nothing, really. (*Slight pause.*) You know, I dunno, but maybe, I'm getting the idea that . . . I think for all of us, it's been a long day and, and we're here to talk *business*, and, well, maybe cos we ain't started yet, its getting us a bit worked up.

Paul and **Samuel** *look at each other and immediately burst out laughing.*

Samuel   This greyhound's really got a way of making us know what he's after.

Paul (*to* **Samuel**)   You know, Simmy, he's married? And I mean his wife, you see a woman like that, it makes perfect sense, I mean, she's something special.

Samuel   Any kiddies?

Simon   A son, twelve on Monday, big man he's gonna be.

Samuel   Jesus. (*To* **Paul**.) So what happened to you then?

Paul   What?

Samuel   You been outdone by your own cousin.

Paul   He's settled. I, on the other hand −

Samuel   Yeah, I know, you're fucked up and you have emotional problems, yet the ladies, nonetheless, can't get enough, can they?

Paul   No, they can't − they all love me.

Samuel   Yes, yes, how true. You surprise me every day. (*Long pause.*) But anyway . . . enough dicking! Come on. Why am I here? (*Slight pause.*) I mean, I'm happy to have you lot rolling over with my humour all evening, but if I stay here I'm gonna freeze to death, my fingers are fucking lollipops.

Paul   Well, here's what it is. (*Pause.*) He must've had an interview up in Thamesmead.

Samuel   OK, I'm listening.

Paul   But they wouldn't let him have the interview. Guess why?

Samuel   Why?

Paul   They thought he was foreign.

Pause. **Samuel** *starts laughing.*

Simon   What?

Samuel   Sorry, friend, but you kinda look foreign.

Slight pause. **Simon***, incredibly angry, looks at* **Samuel***.*

Samuel   No, I'm jokin'. (*To* **Paul***.*) Guy can't take a joke, you should've told me. (*Feigning serious.*) No, me? I don't see colour . . . unless I'm lookin for a porno. Can't afford to be colour blind sometimes, it affects the enjoyment.

Simon   Well, I had the interview.

Samuel   So, you got the job? Is it a good job? Will you enjoy it? – Actually, why the fuck am I here? He's got a job.

Simon   No, I ain't got a job. I didn't stay, I walked out of there. I knew there were better options on the table after speaking to Paul.

Samuel   Ah, is that so?

Simon   More chance making money in a quicker space of time.

Samuel   Uh-huh. So, you want the cash pretty quick?

Simon   Well, who don't? Suits me better, obviously, depending on how I make it.

Samuel   Well, we don't grow it on trees. Wish we did, but still it's pretty quick and it's pretty clean. And actually when you see it all piled up it looks quite pretty too.

Simon   Sounds perfect, can't wait to see it for myself.

Samuel   Can't wait to show you. (*To* **Paul***.*) One thing . . . Criminal record, what's it read like?

Simon   None.

Samuel   Don't kid me, you must have, we're in fucking Deptford.

Simon   I'm clean.

Samuel   OK, but what if I check you out? As a potential employer it wouldn't be so nice to find out that you're telling me lies, you know what I'm saying.

Simon Ask Paul, he knows about me. (*To* **Paul**.) You know about me, don't you?

Paul I know about him – he's clean.

Samuel How clean?

Paul Fairy fucking Liquid.

Samuel Fine. What he says, it's on you. Your responsibility.

Paul No sweat.

Samuel And your licence.

Paul Even cleaner, mate.

Samuel Right, OK, but it's probably fake –

Paul No, it ain't.

Samuel Where'd you get it from? Let me see it.

Simon It's not fake, I been on the buses, the last ten years.

Samuel You been . . . ? (*To* **Paul**.) He's been on the buses?

Paul He's been on the fucking buses.

Samuel Oh . . . Oh right, oh right . . . Sorry. Let's start again . . . Let's just say some lads lie a lot so I ask a lot of questions. (*Pause.*) . . . And so, you've been driving buses for so long you must be able to handle Tippers, low-loaders, shit like that?

Simon Box vans, tri-axles, sleepers, artics, you name it, anything you put in front of me.

Samuel (*to* **Paul**) I like this guy!

Paul See, what did I tell you? Would I bring you round to waste time? This is my cousin we're talking about.

Samuel OK, thank your cousin, he picks good people . . . I expect us to get on well, just don't ask too much questions . . . What else can I tell you . . . Yes, motorways, you must know you way around and shit? We wouldn't need to baby you through it all?

Simon   But I don't expect to be on the motorways.

Samuel   Of course you fucking will.

Simon   It's just a local minicab firm.

Samuel *looks confused.*

Paul   No, Simon –

Simon   But I tell you what, I'll make it easy on you guys . . .
Give me a couple shifts, see how the customers like the way
I drive, regular customers. I know all the short cuts around
here, so I'll save on petrol, increase your profits.

Samuel   What the fuck are you talking about?

Simon   Minicabbing?

Paul   Si . . .

Simon   Yeah?

Paul   The minicab thing is not what we're talking about.

Simon   It's not?

Paul   No.

Simon   Oh, OK, but –

Paul   Something more long-distance, Si.

Simon   Long-distance, right . . . As in – ? OK, well, that's no
problem. I ain't driven long distances for a few months, but it's
no problem.

Samuel (*seriously*)   What the fuck is this?

Paul   Sam, now hold on a sec.

Samuel   Is this a fucking wind-up?

Paul   It's cool, it's cool. Trust me. (*To* **Simon**.) Si, listen, cuz,
I ain't told you all the details yet.

Samuel   So start fucking telling him. I had other options and
you're bringing me here?

Paul   Si, you're gonna be crossing borders, stuff like that. Driving certain things for us.

Simon   What's gonna be the cargo? Drugs?

Samuel   Do I look like I'm ever fucking involved with drugs?

Simon   Well, I don't know.

Paul   No drugs.

Simon   So what then?

Paul   Nothing out the ordinary.

Samuel   Nothing . . . just people.

Simon   What d'you mean, people?

Samuel   Illegals? Aliens? Call 'em what you want. People from outer space. Load them up, drive them in. What's the problem? You want this job?

Simon   You what? (*He looks at* **Paul** *in confusion.*)

Paul   You can do it, Si, it's nothing big.

Simon   . . . So wait, you're telling me I didn't even get a look-in in a job today cos of these fucking foreigners, and you wanna bring more of them over here?

Samuel   Well, I bet you must've noticed how many immigration law firms we have in the area. It's no surprise that they're on every street corner, now, is it?

Simon   You actually make money out of this? The population's out of control as it is!

Paul   Think it over, Si.

Simon   Paul, no, I've got integrity! I thought you did too –

Samuel   You've got integrity? You're fucking broke! What's your integrity gonna do for you?

Simon   Paul, I got into arguments today with my wife, you know why? Cos I was convincing her that what I was doing was driving a minicab, and you want me to be part of this bullshit?

Paul   Hey, come on, Si . . .

Samuel   You know what your problem is, pal? You read the *Sun* too much.

Simon   What d'you say to me?

Samuel   Don't play fucking dumb, lad, you heard me.

Simon   Listen, don't make me put you outside this house.

Samuel   You're lucky I'm even here, you fucking arsehole.

Paul   . . . Come on, look at the real picture. No immigrants have ever hurt nobody, have they?

Samuel   That's right. You should listen to your cousin. Who's gonna mop up after everybody, huh? Mend the roads, look after the old, huh? (*Slight pause.*) The country's fucking lazy. In denial. Believe me, people need immigrants, you think you don't need them. Only bad thing is, you get too much, it temporarily fucks with the national sense of self. But that's all right, just take the Queen out and give her a whirl round town in her fucking Rolls-Royce, or put her on telly, it's sorted, we're fine! (*Slight pause.*) Plus anyway, I know men, some react in different ways. The government goes down the pan, and some men, they just grow their hair long, or dye it, or worse, start looking like Annie Lennox, get all androgynous, you know what I'm saying? Start socially rebelling through their appearance. But the common-sense man, all he does, he just sticks his two fingers up and says sod this, he takes what he can and heads off to Malaga . . . And that's a good thing, make a bit of money, so when the shit hits the fan, you'll be loaded in a sunny country somewhere.

Simon   You know, you're so full of shit.

Samuel *pulls out a large wad of twenty-pound notes, at least five thousand pounds. He puts it on the table.*

Samuel   Exactly – full of it.

Simon   And what? Is that supposed to entice me?

Samuel (*to* **Paul**)   You got five minutes. You either come back with my money or he takes it. I'll be waiting in the car.

He walks towards the door.

Simon   Hey! What about your money?

Samuel   Yeah, just don't spend it all at once.

He exits.

Simon   Hey, you take it! (*He walks to the table and picks up the money.*) Take it! I don't want it!

He moves to the door to follow **Samuel***, but sees that he's already left. He stops and turns to* **Paul***.*

Paul   Simon!

Simon   What the fuck is this, Paul?

Paul   Well . . . now look, just calm down, all right?

Simon   I'm not keeping this, fuck sake. How stupid am I? (*He is about to throw the money out of the door.*)

Paul   Look, just stop!

Simon *stops, he turns round.*

Paul   Look, look, look what's in your hands right now.

Simon *takes notice of the amount of money.*

Paul   Look, right or wrong, answer me. Isn't there a fine line between doing a crime, and just watching it happen?

Simon   This fine line can put me in prison.

Paul   Yeah, I mean, but look, is it bad? Is it? If so, who says? And why? What? Cos it hurts the economy? Cos we're not going through the system? Paying taxes? . . . And what? Aren't crimes happening in this country all the time? Aren't they? And don't we just keep quiet most of the time? (*Slight pause.*) I mean . . . some men, some men, they buy their way into the House of fucking Lords, the old school way, with a brown paper bag in a parking lot, you know what I mean? . . . But the thing is . . . they get away with it! (*Slight pause.*) Sometimes you just gotta close your eyes and hold on to what's gonna keep your head above water, even if it burns holes in your hands. There's just no room for morality, just take hold of what's in your hands.

Simon (*noticing just how much money he is holding*)   This is a lot of money . . . what the hell am I gonna do with all this?

Paul   You see . . . Now don't you feel good to be able to ask yourself that question? (*Pause.*) . . . Think about your kid, yourself, your wife . . . You gotta ask yourself what you want. (*Slight pause.*) So go on, off the top of your head.

Simon   What?

Paul   What d'you want?

Simon   I dunno . . . I dunno . . . I'm thinking, maybe going to Florida or something.

Paul   Now, why you wanna go all the way to Florida for?

Simon   Family holiday.

Paul   A what?

Simon   I ain't been able to take the family nowhere further than Pontins, and that's been with collecting bus vouchers.

Paul   Well, it's there, ain't it?

Simon   I know that, but –

Paul   It's there! You wanna go Florida? Personally I think it's a stupid idea, but you could go, right now, tomorrow! You have the option, Simon! And options are all that we fight for in life. Options! Options to do something! And there's no black man in this part of London who can say that he's got options, is there?

From outside, the car horn beeps repetitively.

Simon   I'm gonna go down there and knock that guy out if he keeps making that noise.

Paul Hey, look at me . . . Look at me. What's the problem? (*Pause.*) Is the wife gonna give you stick? Don't tell her.

Simon I don't lie to my wife, man.

Paul Come on, you're not lying – I mean, this is for her, she just doesn't understand that yet.

Simon I know, but . . .

Paul I got the minicab office? Just tell her you're doing cabbing . . .

Simon But I don't wanna be bringing people in, man.

Paul But you don't have to speak to them, you won't even know who they are. Driving, that's all you'll be doing. Putting your foot on the gas, and moving forward.

The car horn beeps again, repetitively.

Paul You can hear them? These guys, in their minds, they want you involved. I mean, I'm doing a lot, a hell of a lot to get them around . . . I mean, you don't wanna do it . . . OK, fuck it, give me the money.

He takes it out of **Simon**'s *hand.*

Paul I'll go somewhere else, there's some other guys down the road, let them make themselves thousands . . . They can have it, let them have it, instead of family, instead of giving it to you! (*He slams the money on the table.*) Look at it! What is it? Bad money? Good money? It's only bad money when it ain't yours! (*He smiles. Pause.*) And I'll tell you now, no amount of voting or giving any kind of tax payments to a bunch of untrustworthy fuckers is gonna get you a better life . . . Fuck voting, fuck tax, fuck anything that ain't gonna benefit you. Let other people do that. Cos I tell you, when everything's privatised and you can't even take your sick kid to the hospital without donating a kidney, you won't be the one crying on the streets.

Simon I've known you a long time, Paul, I have, I just . . .

The car horn gives another sustained beep.

Paul   Just think about it . . . We wouldn't be throwing down all this money on you if we didn't think it was worth it . . . But you gotta commit! . . . I mean, look at your son. Put yourself in his eyes, see what he sees . . . A poor black man in this country ain't nothing, friend, and soon as he sees that, he'll lose all respect for you, and himself!

Simon   OK, fuck it!

Paul   You're gonna do it?

Simon   Yeah, I'll do it, just one time for now.

Paul   You're gonna do it?

Simon   I'll do it!

Paul   You're gonna fucking do it?

Simon   Yes! I'll! Fucking! Do it!

Paul *instantly embraces* **Simon.** *There is a knocking on the wall from* **George**'s *flat.*

Paul (*shouting through the wall*)   Shut the fuck up, you old cunt! (*To* **Simon.**) You motherfucker! . . . Hey, you! Don't ever make me wait so long for anything. Fucking yes! (*Slight pause.*) Now you cool?

Simon   Yeah, I'm cool . . . I think so.

Paul   We need you tomorrow.

Simon   Tomorrow?

Paul   What the fuck, we don't waste time. There's money to be made, you won't miss that.

Simon   Let them go, why don't you stay . . . I might need to know the route, get used to the van, stuff like that.

Paul   Si, I already left this house ten minutes ago . . . Just come see me in the morning, I'll give you the route, set you up.

Pause. He heads for the door, then stops and turns.

Look, some things are just worth the sacrifice.

He exits. Long pause.

Simon *lets out a big sigh and looks at the money. He takes a few steps back; he looks at it again. He moves the beer bottles out of the way,. He then begins clearing the table, putting the bottles in the bin. He then stops and takes a look at the wall, the same place* **Paul** *had inspected earlier. He puts his hand on the wall and considers replastering it. He goes back to the table and picks up the money, flicking his hands through it, then putting it in his back pocket. He takes it out and slams it on the table. He is again distracted, imagining. His thoughts are growing by the second. He begins measuring the dimensions of the room with his hands, sizing up everything. His vision is getting bigger. He imagines new sofas, a new table. He is sizing up a new living room, a new house. Gradually he begins to smile and, being caught up in the possibilities, he begins to laugh to himself. He can't believe how lucky he is.*

Slow fade.

Act Two

Scene One

The weekend is over. It is Monday, three in the afternoon, and in that short space of time some parts of the flat have been revamped.

Marsha *is dressed in an orange-and-blue Iceland supermarket uniform. Her hair is tied up. She is standing on a small stepladder pinning up birthday decorations on the wall.* **George**, *the next-door neighbour, aged seventy-six, stands watching her. In his hand he holds a birthday present.*

Marsha   You didn't have to get him anything, you know that.

George   I know, I know, I wanted to, plus anyway he'd think I was cruel.

Marsha   Well, he thought I was cruel for making him go to school this morning. The way he kept carrying on, you would've thought I was sending him to his death.

She steps off the stepladder. They both stand looking at the birthday decorations.

What d'you think?

George   Looks great . . . In fact, I was gonna say that as soon as I came in here. Done a good job of the place, you have. And I'm not just talking about the decorations. Makes Buckingham Palace look like Skid Row.

Marsha   Yeah, right . . . Apart from the decorations, I'm not impressed at all . . . (*Slight pause.*) And please, stop being so nice, or else I'll come to your house every day and sit there until you're sick of the sight of me.

She takes the present from him. Pause.

And don't stand there like a cactus either, take a seat.

George (*laughing*)   All right, all right.

Marsha *pulls out a chair for him. Pause.*

Marsha   The amount of years you've lived here, George, are you still in love with the building?

George   Was living on the other side of the market when they built it. Was one of the first lot to move in here at the time. (*Slight pause.*) I remember you had all the brickies around here up in arms, the building methods they used . . . Cutting corners and things like that, saying it's all modern building methods. This building ain't really supposed to be lasting no longer than fifty years or so.

Marsha   It'll probably crumble around us any day now . . . (*Pause.*) You must still love it, though.

George   I hate it.

Marsha (*embarrassed at a sudden thought*) . . . You sure it's not since we moved here? The amount of noise.

George   Oh, quiet. I don't hear a thing.

Marsha   Oh, shut up, George, come on . . .

George   It's true, I never hear a thing, and no loud noises never did bother me anyways. I'm deaf.

Marsha   You're not deaf,

George   Well, if I'm not now, I will be tomorrow, or if not tomorrow, the day after. And if I can still bloody hear anything by then I'd be dead, so what does it matter?

Marsha   Don't say that, you're gonna be around for another hundred years.

George   And what's so great about that?

Pause.

Marsha   You want a cup of tea while you wait for him?

George   No, I'll be all right, thanks.

Marsha   You'll be waiting for forever, you know that. If you want my opinion, don't waste your time.

George   Ah, but I don't want your opinion, it's all negative.

Marsha   Well, he's a child.

George   And so are you.

Marsha   I might be a child, but he's even more of a child.

George   Marsha, you should record what you just said – it sounds stupid.

Marsha   No, I mean, I can accept that I can be immature, because I know I'm not perfect. And anyway, I've already thought that maybe there is something I'm not quite understanding with him . . . (*Slight pause.*) I mean, even this morning, I woke up earlier than him, and I thought, maybe, being the grown-up, I'll – who knows, try talking. And what happened? Well, I suggested that I make him breakfast before he started this new job. This job which he won't tell me anything about. And trust me, for me . . . that was a gigantic gesture, seeing as I've done absolutely nothing wrong . . . Well, guess what he says? He had the cheek to mumble under his breath that if I really understood him, I would know that he never eats breakfast. Can you believe that? (*Slight pause.*) What a waste of time? And I mean, forgive me that I'm not used to dealing with the non-communicative types either. The types that prefer to stay bottled up and only occasionally blurt out a few jumbled messages, which, by the way, you're supposed to decode. (*Slight pause.*) I mean, if I was such a specialist at decoding the confused mixed messages he throws out at me, I'd be in Vauxhall working for the Ministry of Defence. I'd just tell them that I'm a qualified code-breaker. And if they wanted my CV then I'd just tell them to look at whose mixed childish messages I've been decoding for the last ten years . . . They'd give me a job straight away, and probably make a film about me.

George   You know he's at a crossroads, so why crucify the lad about it?

Marsha   Because there's no excuse for mouthing off the way he does. Is there? Don't you hear him?

George   Oh, I hear him.

Marsha   It should be me who's shouting . . . I'm the one who's working in bloody Iceland. Putting what I want to do on hold.

George   Yes, lovely Iceland.

Marsha   And it's not the worst job, but I'm better than that.

George   So what do you want to do?

Marsha   Nothing, just find a way for us to start communicating properly.

George   No – for yourself, you twit.

Marsha   Oh, you mean me? Well . . . (*She thinks.*) Go back to college. Those first few months, I loved it.

George   Well, you're very giving, Marsha, but for your own sanity maybe you should start thinking about yourself, and what you want out of things.

Marsha   Well, the way things are going I might have to.

Pause.

George   You know, my memory's awful, but his shouting . . . It reminds me of being a kid, after the war, was about fifteen, and you had all the young servicemen coming back with legs missing, or blind. It was summer and every time they walked down the street, you'd hear people cheering, they were heroes . . . But when everything quietened down, and a few years passed and nobody was giving them much attention no more, you had them screaming into the night like ghosts. Like Simon, their frustration of being ignored all the time, some people don't know how to deal with it.

Simon *enters. He is in a pleasant mood. He is holding a plastic bag.*

Simon   Mr Manning!

George   Sir, how are you?

Simon   Me? How am I? . . . Feeling good. (*As if thinking about it for the first time.*) Very good . . . Now, what you up to? Chatting up my wife?

George   Ah, she's already mine, you've been gone too long!

Simon   Well, be warned, she comes with migraines. Don't you, honey? (*He laughs.*)

Marsha *looks at* **George**.

George   You look bright!

Simon   George, my boy, funny you say that, I think it's a posture thing, that's all it is . . . I been walking around today, back straight! Head as far off the ground as possible.

George   I have to try it, hey?

Simon   You should! It'll make you feel great. And you can't take that feeling for granted. You see, George, cos there's things in this world that bring you down, and I just figured it out. You can't be going up in the world at a fast rate if you got an opposite force working on you to bring you down. And maybe that's why some people don't achieve nothing, because they aren't aware of the forces around them, they don't make the right choices. For example, a man would say, ah fuck it, I can't cross the river because the bridge is broken, but a smart man would improvise, he'd find a solution, make a bridge out of branches if he had to. (*Slight pause.*) I think that about half the human race is just full of excuse-makers, while the real people, the doers, are the ones carrying the rest of the human race on their shoulders, even if they get persecuted for it.

Marsha   So you've turned into a prophet?

Simon (*smiling*)   Baby, you know you look pretty today. (*Pause.*) You see, I tell her I love her . . .

Marsha   George wants to speak to you.

Simon   About what? Am I in trouble?

He moves to the CD player and takes a CD out of the bag he is holding.

Marsha   Don't take the piss.

Simon   OK, well, I'll be with you in a sec, George. It's just that I've been in Lewisham all day looking for a particular

song . . . I'm interested to see what all the hype is about, with
my son and these old long-dead musicians. (*He delicately puts the
CD in the player.*) Right . . . let's hear what it's all about.

*He presses play. Gershwin's Prelude No. 1 plays. He listens, trying to
gauge the rhythm.*

This ain't so bad . . . OK, I can see it, I'm getting it . . .

As the music's tempo increases he loses a sense of the rhythm.

What's wrong with the CD player?

Marsha   It's fine, that's how it's supposed to sound.

Simon   Sounds like a gypsy's nightmare.

Marsha   Well, that's what he likes.

Simon   I know he likes it . . .

George   Probably you should listen to some Glenn Miller.

Simon (*caught up, listening to the music*)   Huh, who?

George   Miller. Big band.

Simon   Yeah, I should. (*Slight pause. He looks again at the CD.*)
But you know, I'm happy my son listens to this stuff . . .
I mean, it's his music, and I don't dislike it or nothing . . . Just,
I haven't had the time to get into it, know all the songs. (*Pause.*)
And I'm happy him listening to this stuff, but as long as he
don't turn into one of them different types of people, you
know what I mean?

Marsha   How can you talk about your own son like that?

Simon   Well, it's true, he's interested in a lot of stuff that he
don't tell me about it.

Marsha   You don't like the things he likes, that's why.

Simon   What you mean? I love his stuff. I mean this music,
it's good . . . You know what I mean? (*Slight pause. To* **George**.)
You know what it is, George, I blame this country . . .

Marsha   Oh, here we bloody go again.

Simon   It's true, people all sectioned off into little ghettos everywhere. And what happens is, the people with money, they like something they make it special and hide it from everyone else, and my son, cos he's at that school he's mixing with those types.

Marsha   George hasn't got all day, Simon.

Simon   All right, all right. (*Slight pause.*) Well, OK. (*Pause.*) So, George, what is it? What you wanna see me about?

George   Well, see, Si . . . Why don't you sit down for a sec?

Simon   OK. (*Sitting down.*) What can I help you with?

George   Well, you see, Simon, . . . I don't want you to take any offence with what I'm gonna say.

Simon   Oh, I won't take any, depends what you say, don't it? (*He laughs.*)

Pause.

George   It's something about me.

Simon   Yeah, and I'm all ears.

George   . . . I was talking about this flat today with Marsha, and I realised that I'm not happy living here.

Marsha   George? I thought you said were happy here.

George   No, please, Marsha, let me speak . . . Now, Simon, I've been speaking to my social worker, a nice young lady who agrees with me that I should think about moving into somewhere smaller, with a lift, and with less noise, more clean air.

Simon   I mean, what? Are we making too much noise? Is that boy making too much noise for you?

Marsha   Simon, it's you, no one else.

George   No, it's no one . . . I'm happy . . . but I'm just getting on, I'm an old git – come on, look at me. Now look, over the years my house has picked up a lot of value, and I'm gonna sell it.

Simon   Good on you.

George   But I don't wanna sell it to any developers, and
they've been putting all their letters through my door every day
so they can knock it down and turn it into something fancy.
Now it's all well and good me selling it for a nice old profit, but
if you ask me I'd be happy offering my house over to you lot
for a price you can afford, and then if you buy it sooner or
later when they decide to knock all the houses down and turn
everything all fancy, who's gonna be laughing? Cos all the
other housing association people, they're all getting moved out,
all the locals. But you can just stick your fingers up at them
and say, pay ten times the amount.

Long pause. **Simon** *stares at* **George**. *He laughs.*

Simon (*putting his hand on* **George**'s *shoulder*)   Get out of here –
you're losing it.

George   No, I'm being very serious, Simon, ain't it a great
thing?

Simon   George, hold on . . . Let me ask you somethin'.

George   All right, go on.

Simon   Are you dead?

Marsha   Simon!

Simon   Well, are you? (*To* **Marsha**.) Now let me ask.

George   Well, I'm not.

Simon   So what are you saying? . . . You think you won't
need the money that you'll make on the house for yourself?

George   Yes, but it doesn't really matter, all that money, I'll
never use it.

Simon   So what? It's yours, it's profits, you make it, you keep it.

George   Yes, of course, but that's not the only important
thing, is it? What kind of life are you having if you're only
chasing penny after penny all day? And being where you are
now, I know what it's all about, it's hard . . . I know how hard
it is to focus on what's important.

Simon   You know how hard it is, do you?

George   The cost of living, it goes up and up, never coming down. And if you don't own your house and all your money goes to the housing association for nothing, it ain't doing you no good.

Marsha   Would you really do that for us, George?

George   I'm saying it, ain't I?

Marsha   Simon, look at what's being offered – it's fantastic.

George   Marsha, you've always taken care of me for such a long time now, and I'm not gonna forget about things like that.

Simon   Wait, hold on a minute! Now George, I don't mean this in no bad way, but you know what? Sometimes, just sometimes I think you should try and do something else instead of just listening to what goes on inside this house. God's sake, I mean, I know the walls are thin.

Marsha   Simon, show some respect!

Simon   Stay out of this, hon!

George   Now, I might not be saying exactly what I mean, but –

Simon   George, the cost of living? You know how hard it is? What else can you mean by that? . . . It's something you can either deal with or you can't! (*He takes money out of his pocket.*) Now, do I look as if I can't cope with the cost of living? Do I?

George   There's more to life you should be appreciating, son.

Simon   A lot more about life? George, me and your lives are totally different! There's nothing you can understand about me.

George   And what's that supposed to mean?

Simon   Well, for one, you've never experienced the problems I've had. Look at yourself and look at me.

George   That don't mean nothing. I can step in your shoes just like you can step in mine.

Marsha   Simon! Please!

Simon (*to* **Marsha**)   You call my name out again I'm gonna get real mad with you! (*Slight pause. Getting up.*) I'm sorry George, thank you for coming over and for offering all this stuff . . . but I'm perfectly fine. I don't need no handouts.

George   This is not a handout.

Simon   Oh, it is.

George   Now, Simon, I've said there's things in life −

Simon   − I know everything about life.

George (*shouting*)   What I've forgotten you haven't even bloody well learnt yet!

Marsha   George, please.

Simon   I won't take anything from no man.

Marsha   Why wouldn't you take anything? You don't have anything.

Simon   Well, I don't give a damn. This is my house, and I decide what goes on in it.

Marsha   No, this is not even your house, OK?! It belongs to the Deptford housing! And we're three months behind in rent and could be asked to leave any time they want.

Simon   No, we won't! We're fine, I've got it covered.

Marsha   Sorry?

Simon   You heard what I said, I've paid the rent arrears all up. Went there, paid it all up today.

Marsha   With what?

Simon   I've made plans, that are starting to come together, that's all you need to know.

George   I've heard about the kind of plans you've got and they're going to put you in a lot of trouble.

Marsha   George, what are you talking about? . . . Simon?

Simon   He's not saying anything. He's senile.

George   Marsha, I'm gonna go. (*Getting up.*) And I'm gonna pull you up on something, Simon . . . You saying that there's no difference between us.

Simon   Oh, come on, you're an English white man.

George   English? White? Most nights if Marsha ain't kind enough to help me out of my chair at night, who does? What does English and white do for me then? I'm left to sit there uncomfortable till the home helps come at midday. It's not a colour thing, man! It's money, it's importance! And we're just not important enough . . . both of us.

Simon (*getting up*)   George, I've got things to do.

George   Simon, I want you to think about what I'm offering.

Simon   I don't need to think about it

George   Well, still, give it a day, sit on it for a couple days.

Simon   I said no!

George *slowly gets up.* **Marsha** *helps him.*

Marsha   George, I'm sorry, you should have told me. I'm sorry that this stupid, ignorant . . .

George   It's quite all right, Marsha, don't worry. (*To* **Simon**.) I had good friends arrive on that *Britannia Windrush*, who knew what struggle was, working the rail things and all that when no one else was. Who'd stand in queues in the rain day and night looking for work. They knew how to throw away pride, son.

Simon   Yeah, OK, George, take it easy . . .

Marsha (*helping* **George** *to the door*)   George, I'll be over in an hour, OK?

George *exits.*

Marsha *returns. She stares at* **Simon.**

Simon   You believe that! Think I'm gonna take his house? (*Slight pause.*) I'm gonna have to make sure when I finish doing this place up, I'm gonna put a fucking extra wall on that place.

Marsha Why d'you have to talk to him like that?

Simon Like what?

Marsha Like what? You don't even know, do you?

Simon (*sarcastically*) No, I don't.

Marsha Everyone. Everyone! Has to wait until you're ready. You're so proud. And proud of what? You're the reason why we haven't got anywhere, why I'm made to feel so desperate and cheap! Doing things I hate! . . . Sometimes I look at you and I don't see you any more.

Simon Maybe you need some glasses. (*He reaches into his pocket and throws some money onto the table.*) Here, take it. Go buy yourself some.

Marsha Oh yes! Look at it. You get all the strength you need now, don't you? Crying like a baby for the last three months and suddenly, you're a new man! You turn down a perfectly good offer because you've got a bunch of paper to throw at everyone. That's all it is, paper! And you put that over everyone who cares for you. You criticise your son, you insult me! You humiliate George! Why? (*Pause.*) You're a stubborn man, a hollow shell, washed up, and the life inside, it's just out to sea, struggling in the blackness and the night.

Simon (*sitting down*) I want you to make a note of this . . . (*Slight pause. He pulls out a bus ticket from his pocket.*) I took a bus to Lewisham. Two pounds I had to pay for a bus ride. Write it down . . . The date at the top of the page, and then say . . . 'Dear Ken, it costs two pounds to get on a bus three stops. Well, I'm gonna get enough money to buy a bus,' you tell him. Putting the price up every ten minutes. When I started driving the buses, I was charging twenty-five pee.

Marsha I don't care about your stupid buses!

Simon And I don't wanna hear what you gotta say! With your nagging.

Marsha You're putting our lives at risk!

Simon So what do you want me to say? You think I'm just selfish? Thinking of myself? Then what d'you want me to say?

Marsha *wipes a tear away from her cheek.*

Simon Yeah, go on, cry, that's all you seem to do. (*Long pause.*) And why you even got that old man coming here for? You knew what he was up to. Trying to say I'm the same as him? You think my life ain't more important than that old fucking . . .

Marsha And what makes you decide if someone's life is less or more important than yours?

Simon Oh please, look at him!

Marsha (*beginning to rip down the decorations*) I've had it. I've had it!

Simon (*grabbing hold of her*) Now, come on now, what you doing?

Marsha I don't wanna be in this house any more, I can't do it any more.

Simon Well, go on, the door's there. Get out, get out, then, don't be here.

He grabs hold of her and tries to drag her to the door. She resists. He gives up. Pause.

Can you, just for once, just be a little happy for me. (*Slight pause.*) I've taken an opportunity that was presented to me, and for the first time in a year I feel like I could explode I'm so happy (*Long pause.*) Baby, come on, I lived in fear, every day I was scared, every day I was scared that I wouldn't be strong enough for you and Anthony when you needed me most. But for once, for once I can put my fingers on life. My senses are so sharp. (*Pause.*) Cos, baby, before today, I was on a downward spiral, baby, falling. I was falling. I felt like . . . I'd go to work, and at the end of the day I'd get off the bus, come home and I'd feel like a dot, insignificant. And I used to take off my uniform and I'd crash on the bed. And I'd hit the covers, but you know, I'd keep falling and I couldn't stop. I'd fall through the bed. I'd feel myself fall though the floor of this flat, through the ceiling beneath, until I reached the earth and the bones and the mud, and all the dead things. And I'd open my eyes and try to hold on to something, but it's like I'm invisible cos I just keep falling, through the middle of the earth, right through to the other side . . . And there's nothing for me to hold on to. I just fall into darkness, right out into space. There was nothing on this whole earth that I could hold on to. (*Slight pause.*) I had to shake myself up, and tell myself to stop thinking the way I'm thinking. (*He takes out money from his pocket.*) Look now, there's opportunities. I'm . . . I'm able to feel some control in my life.

Marsha   But why is it money has to make all the difference?

Simon (*with sincerity*)   Isn't everything all about money, baby? I mean, am I doing something wrong? You tell me . . . Is it a lie that when I look and see this money in my hand, I feel good? Why you so mad at me? Why?

Long pause. **Marsha** *goes and picks up the few decorations she ripped down.*

Marsha   Having a mortgage on a house and at a price we can afford, that's control, that's feeling good. Now when someone offers you that, it's a blessing, you don't throw it away.

Simon   I didn't take it, cos we don't need it . . . I've got bigger plans.

Marsha   And what are they?

Simon   What does it matter?

Marsha   It matters, if you want to take our lives in a direction I'm not aware of.

Pause.

Simon   It's basic cab work.

Marsha   Cab work, oh wow!

Simon   Yes, that's the starting point.

Marsha   God, simple jobs just pay so well these days, don't they?

Simon (*getting up, not listening*)   Right, come on, I'm tired and fed up of talking . . . Now I'm gonna do what I came here to do . . . it's my son's birthday, for God's sake, and I only came to drop something. (*Pause.*) And when I get back, I want you to change your attitude, put some faith in me.

Abruptly he walks out of the house. After a period of time he returns carrying a large rectangular box – **Anthony***'s present. He stops in the middle of the room. The box is heavy; he struggles.*

Long pause. They both look at each other. **Simon***'s struggle continues as he tries to carry the box into the room.*

Marsha   In eighteen years of knowing you, Simon, you've never lied to me.

Simon (*without looking at her*)   You just gonna stand there, you gloomy thing? You gonna help me with this or what?

Marsha   How much was it?

Simon   What's price got to do with it? . . . It was cheap.

Marsha   What's Paul got you doing, Simon?

Simon (*stepping back to look at the present, not listening*)   . . . It's for professionals. I told the guy at the store, that I gotta have the best thing they got. (*Pause.*) Don't you like what I got him?

Marsha   . . . I need to lie down.

As she walks away, **Simon** *holds on to her gently.*

Simon (*reluctant to let go of her*)   Baby, come on now, can you just loosen up and relax? (*Pause. Still holding her. Hesitant.*) . . . I think about you, you know, you wouldn't think I do, but I do. When I'm out on the road sometimes. I stare out of the windscreen and I look right into the distance. To me you're like that white line in the middle, keeping me focused.

Marsha   Just tell me what you do. And don't tell me it's minicabbing.

Simon   OK, and I tell you, that would put your mind at ease?

Marsha   Tell me.

Simon   OK, now, apart from minicabbing, which is what I do, believe it or not . . . There were a few odd jobs lying around that I picked up. And the reason why I got all this money is cos the way it works you get paid in advance in this business.

Marsha   And what you're doing, is it legal?

Simon   Baby, you think too bad of people, that's your problem.

Marsha (*after a pause*)   Would you give the money back if I asked you to, as someone who cares a lot about you?

Simon   Give the money back? (*He laughs.*) No. I've already spent it.

Marsha (*holding his hand*) Well, we'll make it back in other ways. Just quit please, don't do this job any more.

Simon (*after a pause, smiling*)   We used to have fun, Marsh. When we was kids, huh? You remember how we first met? . . . I called you over, you remember, I figured you were like a piece of fruit . . . So I called you a tomato cos your skin was soft and I could see the light shining right through you . . . You only let me walk with you five minutes down the road . . . Sometimes I wanna go back to that feeling.

Marsha   I love you too, Simon, but I want you to listen to me. Life's about choices. And I'm begging you please, please.

Simon   I'm not gonna stop until I see everything through, I've already given my word.

Marsha   Simon!

Simon   Get off me now . . . If you love me, you'll accept everything I do.

Paul, *seeing the door open, enters the flat. He stands watching them.*

Paul   The real world is never documented. Look at you two.

Simon *lets go of* **Marsha** *and turns round.*

Simon   Paul?

Paul   Two lovers, look at you guys.

Marsha *quickly wipes the tears from her face.*

Simon   I was just heading back to the office.

Paul   Well, you better get there quick, I just got a call that you've left my fruit and veg out to rot on the side of the road. That's all got to get to Dalston fresh, mate.

Simon   I'll head out there right now.

Paul   You leave my vans on the double yellows it'll cost me fuckloads of money for nothing. (*Pause.*) You gotta be showing more responsibility, Sim, huh? You're messing me up with the whole situation right now. I'm relying on you.

Simon   I'm not even here.

Pau *gives* **Simon** *a pat on the back as he passes to grab his things.*

Paul   How you doing there, Marsh?

Marsha   . . . All right.

Paul   You know, it's always nice to see a couple in love like you two.

Simon (*to* **Marsha**)   Marsha, make him a cup of tea please, babe. (*To* **Paul**.) I'll see you all later.

Simon *exits. Pause.* **Marsha** *heads to the sink and turns on the kettle.*

Paul   You know what? Something just came to me . . . You know what you're like? You're like an image, that's it, that's what came into my head, a photograph. I can see you in my head, and to see you in the flesh, it's such a treat . . .

Pause.

Marsha   How many sugars?

Paul   Oh none, no – one, no – four.

Pause. There is a silence while **Marsha** *makes the tea.*

Paul   Too skinny, need to put on some weight . . . Went to this doctor I know, he ain't trained but knows all the stuff, told me I need to eat a bag of sugar a day. (*Pause.*) You know, I remember when you were a kid, you know that?

Marsha   When?

Paul   When you was about nineteen. You remember me?

Marsha   Vaguely. I figured you weren't coming out of prison.

Pause.

Paul   Oh no, I'm back, I'm here . . . Prison, it's just, it's like sleeping, and sleeping's like being dead if you think about it the right kinda way. Coming outside, it's like waking up again. Things change when you expect everything to be the same. And I mean, look how you all turned out, you've become a grown woman, you got your own house now. I thought you two were just gonna date like all young kids and split up, and now Anthony's always messing around, pressing all the buttons in my car, pretending to drive. (*Pause.*) And as soon as I come in your house, I can smell this smell, you know?

Marsha   What smell?

Paul   The smell of family.

Marsha   What does it smell of?

She brings the cup of tea over to him.

Paul   What does it smell of? . . . People!

Marsha   Well, it's never too late for you, is it?

Paul   For me? . . . Nah, I live too much of an uneventful life.

Marsha   With a nice car and house, no doubt.

Paul   Ahh . . . I bought that car with some of the salary I made in prison.

Marsha   Oh, really? Paid whilst in prison? Wonderful.

Paul   I was a librarian for some years – used to help all the others with the City and Guilds, and HNC forms, stuff like that.

Marsha   Well, it seems to have been a worthwhile cause.

Paul   Yes, well, I've changed now, it changed me. Never get involved in a lifestyle on the edge. Just feels good to have a business of my own, doing well.

Marsha   And you've been so kind to Simon, giving him a job, haven't you?

Paul   It's a freight company – it's as simple as that. I needed workers and he was around, and he's family.

Marsha   I thought he was working as a minicab driver.

Paul   Oh, yes, yes, the minicab part of the business. Just expanding things here and there, gotta keep the head above water.

Marsha (*mild sarcasm*)   Oh, right. Well, I suppose he's making more money than we're used to. I should be happy. And this time next month, probably sooner, since we're doing so well, we'll be able to realise our ambitions, we've always wanted above all else to have the wall solid gold-plated, you see.

Paul (*slightly confused*)   Suppose it would look all right. Kinda Middle Eastern . . . (*Slight pause. Noticing her sarcasm.*) Aha! . . . I spot a bit of sarcasm . . . (*Slight pause.*) Look, all I can say is, well, work it out. I mean, how do you get to the top of any business? How'd you get the best pay? By working for a stranger who don't look out for your interests? A lot of people in life, they want something but they don't know what they want. Simon knows what he wants and I been giving him some encouragement, throwing him a few extra drinks, more than he'd expect to see, that's all . . . The last thing I wanna see is something to happen to you all. Imagine you having some bailiffs come to your house, saying they ain't leaving unless you give him your fridge or something . . . It happens . . .

Marsha Yeah, well.

Pause.

Paul What can I say? This tea, erm . . . you make very nice tea.

Marsha Thank Tetley. I just pour the water.

Paul It's real weird. I don't think I would've ever been in a situation like this, you know? Being in a flat, sitting at a table, doing normal things. (*Slight pause.*) I had no one to pick me up when I was making mistakes, no tradition passed down . . . You can't hold that against Simon.

Marsha Well, he says you're like a father to him, so there you go.

Paul He says that about me?

Marsha He talks about you all the time.

Paul (*after a pause*) Man, I swear to you right now I'd almost burst out crying. (*Pause.*) Well, hey, I suppose if I don't go back to the business now, I won't be eating tonight . . . (*Long pause. Admiring the decorations on his way out.*) I like the decorations, by the way.

Marsha (*emotionlessly*) Yeah, thanks.

Paul (*stopping and turning round*) Anthony having his big party tonight?

Marsha No, just a small celebration.

Paul Where is he? School?

Marsha Yes.

Paul Where is it?

Marsha Croydon.

Paul You're going all the way to Croydon?

Marsha No, I'll grab him from the station.

Paul   Well, if you want – (*Looking at his watch.*) I've got a few hours spare, if you want I could drive you down . . . It's his birthday after all.

Marsha   No, it's unnecessary.

Paul   I can get there in twenty minutes.

Marsha   Yes, and at that speed, no thanks.

Paul   But you can't let a young guy travel home like that on his birthday, can you? And you know how much the boy loves riding in the Porsche? We could pick him up and go for a spin, he'll love it. (*Pause.*) Come on . . .

Marsha   No.

Paul   You sure now?

Pause.

Marsha   Yes.

Paul   Well . . . fair enough.

Pause.

Marsha   What time is Simon due home from work tonight?

Paul (*looking at his watch*)   No later than ten . . .

Marsha (*standing by the window*)   I believe my son should have a great day.

Paul   Well, if you change your mind we'll give him a call later, he'll come join us.

Marsha   Oh no, he's working. If he wants to feel he's putting food on the table. (*Pause.*) I've had a change of heart, Paul . . . Let's go, it's my son's birthday, let him have what he doesn't usually get.

Paul   Yeah?

Marsha   I said, let's go. Wait for me downstairs . . . I want him to enjoy today, nothing's gonna get in the way.

Paul   You know, Marsh . . . thanks for trusting me.

Marsha   Oh, shut up.

Paul   I'll meet you in the car.

Marsha *stares at the electric keyboard with an air of defiance while she puts her coat on. She exits.*

Lights down.

Scene Two

As 'Rhapsody in Blue' increases to a chaotic volume, the stage remains in total darkness. The time is now 11.30 p.m., and the only light is the mild glow of the street lamps outside, illuminating the room enough to see **Simon** *sitting at the table, looking at the wall. The light in the corridor outside the house switches on: it is* **Anthony** *returning home. He bursts into the room.*

Anthony (*ecstatically*)   Dad! Dad! . . .

Simon *turns to look at* **Anthony**. *He doesn't say anything.* **Anthony** *stands waiting, then quickly runs to the CD player and switches off the music.*

Anthony   You missed it, man, Dad.

Simon   Where were you?

Anthony   Oh, you missed it big time!

Simon   Missed what?

Anthony   Today! Everything!

Simon   What happened?

Anthony   We went out with Uncle Paul, in his car. And it moves so fast it feels like you're flying . . . It's the speed, Dad, and it's so shiny and black, all the other kids were jealous. We flew right past them!

Simon   OK, look, slow down . . . Start again, where did you go?

Anthony   Mum and Uncle Paul picked me up from school.

Simon   OK.

Anthony   And I was coming out of school, and I saw Mum waving at me from the school gate, she was standing next Paul's car. (*Slight pause.*) And everyone was saying to me, wow, is that your dad's car.

Simon   Really?

Anthony   Yeah.

Simon   And what did you say?

Anthony (*apprehensively*)   I said yes, but I didn't mean it.

Simon   But it's not my car.

Anthony   I know, but you said you were gonna get a car like that anyway. (*Slight pause.*) OK, when you get your car, me and you can drive around. And you could pick me up from school next year and let *me* drive you home, how about that?

Simon   You're too young to drive.

Anthony   Oh, Dad!

Simon   Is that all you're gonna talk about? Cars all the time?

Anthony   No . . .

Simon   Come on, it's late. (*Slight pause.*) It's your birthday, you're not supposed to be out of the house so late when we were already supposed to celebrate everything here.

Slight pause. **Anthony** *notices the cake that is resting on the cooker.*

Anthony   Dad, you got a cake!

Simon   Leave it alone . . . Go take your uniform off. Ain't you got school tomorrow?

Anthony   I'm not tired.

Simon   But you will be, so do it. Go put your bedclothes on.

There is a sound coming from the front door. **Marsha** *and* **Paul** *walk into the flat in hysterics.*

Paul (*to* **Marsha**)   You gotta learn to shut a door properly, Marsha! It's no laughing matter . . . Some things, they depreciate in value even quicker than you want them to if you knock 'em so hard.

Marsha   Oh, what are you talking about now?

Paul   That's a good damn car outside!

Marsha   So what? Doors are for closing, so hush up and relax. (*She turns the light on.*) Simon, you're here?

Simon   Where d'you think I'd be? Where'd you go?

Paul (*grabbing hold of* **Anthony** *as he's exiting*)   Went to watch a film, didn't we?

Anthony   Yeah.

Simon   But Paul, why didn't you tell me?

Paul (*to* **Marsha**)   Marsha, I thought you said you left a message on his mobile? (*To* **Simon**.) There's a message on your mobile, son.

Marsha   Didn't you get my message, hon?

Simon   Come on, who you playing games with? My phone didn't ring once!

Marsha   It didn't?

Simon   No, it fucking didn't!

Paul   OK, all right, Sime? (*Slight pause.*) Plus, anyway, the film – it was about the life of some girl boxer. She died and that was it. It was shite. So we left and stopped off in Leicester Square, had some ice cream, no real biggie.

Pause.

Simon   Well, what d'you want me to say? (*To* **Paul**.) Paul, I'm with a woman who don't have standards. No morals . . . Keeps a father away from his son on his birthday. (*To* **Marsha**.) You're a savage.

Paul   Come on, Si.

Simon   Man, you know the kinda women I'm talking about?

Marsha   Paul, would you like a drink? There's a lot of hot air in this room.

Paul   Oh no, thanks, I'm all right. (*Slight pause.*) Truth be told, I'm knackered . . . I'm about to go anyway. Where's that diamond? Lemme say goodnight.

Simon   In his bedroom.

Paul (*walks to the bedroom door; calling out*)   Calling Officer Anthony, requesting backup. (*Slight pause.*) Officer Ant! Two criminals, two IC3s medium height, one male, one female, they're surrounding me, they're about to eat me . . . they're cannibals.

Anthony (*emerging from his bedroom*)   What's IC3 again?

Paul   Never mind. Don't worry about it . . . What took you so long? I would've been killed by now in the real world.

Anthony   No you wouldn't.

Paul   I would, you gotta be fast, think quick . . . act on your toes in the concrete jungle . . . Come, I wanna show you something before I go.

Anthony   What is it?

Paul   Come see. Quit asking questions. Mum and Dad, why does this boy ask so much questions?

He sits down at the table. **Simon** *gets up and looks from a distance. From time to time he watches* **Marsha.** **Paul** *pulls out a coin from his pocket.*

Paul   Now I'm gonna show you something, that I know you've never seen before. I would've shown you earlier but I forgot . . . Are you watching? Are you ready?

Anthony   Yeah, what is it?

Paul   Hold on . . . Now there was a time once when the whole world was fought over silver and gold . . .

Anthony Why's that?

Paul Because it looked good – now shut up and listen . . .
And it was the most precious thing in the world . . . all the
ancient leaders would wear it as a sign of power and status.

Anthony Like the ancient Incas?

Marsha Anthony, let Uncle Paul tell his story.

Paul It's all right . . . Yeah, whoever those guys are. Actually
I used to know a couple of them up in Catford, I think. (*Slight
pause.*) Now anyways, hundreds of years later the sons of these
great rulers, I mean they no longer had the gold, cos all the
white people took it, but they had power and strength because
they'd fought big battles against the Europeans with spears and
knuckledusters against guns and stuff. And they survived . . .
And then years later some of them moved to south London
and you know, basically I'm one of them.

Anthony No, you're not.

Paul I am, my great-great-great-great-great-grandad was a
king, that's why I'm known as the hard man of south London.
I got king's blood in me, ask your dad.

Anthony How can you prove it, though? If you don't have
any proof I won't believe you.

Paul Well, it's about time – I thought you'd never ask . . .
Look, gonna show you how strong I am . . . See, just like my
ancestors I got a jaw like a shark, I can chew anything, any
gold or silver you put in front of me, even a fifty-pence piece.

Anthony No, you can't. Dad, d'you hear that?

Paul Well, OK.

He holds out the coin. **Anthony** *watches in anticipation.*

Paul Now watch me. (*Handing the coin to* **Anthony** *to test.*)
Take a look, fifty pee, right? Try bend it, see what happens, it's
real. Right?

Anthony (*testing it and giving it back*) Yeah, OK.

Paul *takes the coin, bites it and holds it out. The coin appears to have been bitten in half.*

Anthony (*amazed*)   Lemme see, how d'you do that?

Paul *covers the coin with his other hand and blows on it, and when he removes his hand it returns to a full coin.*

Anthony   How'd you do it?

Simon   It's not a real coin.

Paul *flicks the coin to* **Simon. Simon** *catches it. He looks at it.*

Paul   Who says it's not a real coin?

Anthony   How'd you do it? Lemme see it.

He grabs the coin out of **Simon**'s *hand.*

Simon   It's just a trick coin.

Anthony   It's not, it's real.

He tries to bite the coin but it doesn't work. **Paul** *laughs.*

Paul   You want me to show you how to do it?

Anthony   Yeah, go on, show me.

Paul   OK, here, you need to sit down first.

Simon (*to* **Paul**)   What you teaching him, Paul?

Paul   Just a nothing trick. (*To* **Anthony**.) Something so when you go to school tomorrow, at lunchtime, you can have all the people around you blown away . . . But the only thing is, only do it once, no matter who asks you. Don't let no one see it twice or they'll figure it out.

Anthony   OK.

Paul   You sure now?

Simon   You know, to be honest, Paul, I don't really feel comfortable you teaching him things like that . . .

Marsha   Why? What's wrong with it?

Simon (*ignoring her, but answering to* **Paul**)   He'll get known at school as some clown, doing tricks all day, no one will trust him.

Marsha   Don't be so childish.

Simon   I'm just saying how I feel about it, Paul.

Anthony   Oh Dad, I won't.

Simon   No, now that's enough of it.

Paul   Oh come on, Simon, loosen up, huh?

Simon   Look, I've said how I feel. Please respect my wishes.

Paul (*slight pause*)   OK, all right. Fair enough . . .

Anthony   Stupid.

Simon   What'd you say to me, boy?

Anthony   Nothing.

Paul   OK, fine. All right, boy . . . another time, huh?

Anthony *disappointedly gets up. Long pause.* **Simon** *notices everyone looking at him.*

Simon   What you all looking at me like that for?

Marsha   Couldn't you see the child was having fun?

Long pause.

Simon (*to* **Anthony**)   OK, come here then, let me show you how you do it.

Marsha   You don't even know what you're doing –

Simon   Hey, relax, all right . . . I know exactly what I'm doing. (*To* **Paul**.) Let me have the coin, Paul. Let me do it.

Paul (*takes the coin from his pocket and slides it on the table to* **Simon**) Suit yourself, Si, it's nothing important.

Marsha   Simon, you're being absolutely ridiculous.

Simon   I'll do it. Now, Anthony, come here . . . look. Well. *sit down.*

Anthony *sits down at the table. A pause.*

Simon   Now all you do is . . . is.

He fiddles with what he thinks is the correct finger position. He takes a closer look at the coin.

Right, look, it's simple . . . You hold it out and show everybody, right. OK, like this. (*He holds out the coin.*) And then you pretend to bite it, from one end. But what you really do is slide it halfway down your hand. (*He tries to do this himself but the coin drops on the floor.*)

Anthony   But Dad, Uncle Paul bit the coin. I saw it.

Simon   I can assure you, he didn't bite it, it's a trick of the eyes, you *think* you saw him bite it, but he didn't.

Anthony   He did.

Simon (*being unable to perform the trick successfully, he gives up*) Fine, Paul, do it. Show him the damn trick then.

Paul   You almost got it . . .

In a huff of frustration **Simon** *gets up and walks to the window. Pause. Once* **Paul** *starts speaking, he stares back at them.*

Paul (*sitting closely with* **Anthony** *and looking up to* **Simon**) Now your dad's right, it's all about the eyes. (*To* **Simon**.) Ain't that right, Si?

Simon *doesn't respond; instead he lights a cigarette and turns to look out of the window.*

Paul (*to* **Anthony**, *hypnotically*)   . . . It's the eyes . . . Where you look, they'll look. First thing you gotta do, is practice how to distract somebody . . . then, see, you get two coins. (*He pulls out another coin from his pocket.*) One is the fake, one is the real.

He takes the fake coin, bends it in half and gives it to **Anthony**.

Anthony (*playing with the coin, flipping it in half*)   Wow, that's how you do it?

Simon (*turning to look*)   Well, you didn't tell me that, did you?

Paul   What?

Simon   About the fake coin.

Paul   It's not like you gave me a chance to, eh, Sime?

Simon *again diverts his attention back outside. But as soon as* **Paul** *starts talking he turns again and watches them.*

Paul   Then when no one's looking, in a flash you switch the coins over.

He demonstrates with efficient speed. **Anthony** *is amazed.*

Paul   Hiding the first one in between your thumb, like this. And make sure no one sees it . . .

He takes the coin and walks it through with **Anthony**, *holding* **Anthony**'s *hand and placing the coin between his thumb and forefinger.*

Paul   Get used to holding the coin there, and eventually, you'll be able to click your fingers, and everyone will think your hands are empty.

Anthony *practises, but with difficulty.*

Paul   There – you almost got it.

Anthony   Look, I'm doing it. (*He shows* **Marsha**.) Look, cool, innit?

Marsha   Well done, sweetheart.

Anthony (*to* **Paul**)   Can I keep it?

Paul   Of course, mate, it's yours.

Anthony   Really? Yeah!

Paul *nods.*

Anthony   You wait till tomorrow . . . Uncle Paul, this is best present! (*He walks up to* **Simon**.) Dad, let me show you how you do it.

Anthony *tries to perform the trick to a disinterested* **Simon**, *but instead drops the coin on the floor between* **Simon**'s *feet. He reaches down to grab it.*

Simon   Come on, son, stop leaning on me.

Anthony, *in retrieving his coin, accidentally stands on* **Simon**'s *foot.*

Simon   Ouch! You're stepping on my foot.

Anthony *steps back away from* **Simon**.

Marsha (*to* **Simon**)   What's come over you?

Simon   He's stepping all over me.

Anthony   I'm sorry.

Paul   Hey, Si, cheer up, huh?

Simon   What's all the fuss over a bloody coin?

Marsha   Come here, Anthony, don't mind him . . . (*To* **Paul**.) Would you like a drink?

Paul (*getting up*)   No, no . . . I'm gonna be making a move.

Anthony   You going?

Paul   Yeah, I'll have to, I can't keep you up late. There's a lot of planning to do, can never take a day's rest . . . Marsha, it's been a pleasure, I had a good time today . . . first time in a long time. And, Anthony, keep practising. Simon?

Simon   Yeah, I'll see you . . .

Anthony   When you gonna come around again?

Paul   I'll be here all the time.

Suddenly a car alarm goes off.

Shit, is that my car?

He goes to check, and sees that it's his car that has been set off.

Fucksake, having a car like that outside, might as well have a Page Three blonde standing there in her knickers. Bastards, can't keep your car parked anywhere these days. I gotta go! Hey, have a good one. (*He exits.*)

Anthony   I'll come downstairs with you.

Marsha (*to* **Anthony**)   No, you stay here, it's too late. (*To* **Paul**.) See you, Paul.

Anthony   Bye, Paul!

He runs to the window to watch him. Long pause. **Anthony** *yawns and stretches.*

Marsha   Anthony, come here . . .

Anthony *walks to her.*

Marsha   This is the last time, you stay up so late, look at you. (*She runs her hand through his hair.*)

Anthony (*flicking her hand away*)   Leave me alone.

Marsha   Go and wash your face and brush your teeth.

Anthony   Mum, I'll do it in the morning.

Marsha   No, you won't!

Anthony   But I'm too tired now, I wanna sleep.

Marsha   Anthony.

Anthony   OK, OK, I'm going, I'm going. (*He heads for the bathroom.*)

Marsha   And I'll be checking.

Anthony *exits. Long pause.*

Simon   You're so happy, ain't you?

Marsha   About what?

Simon   Don't act so naive.

Marsha   Simon, you're the one who decided that we treat Paul like family! That's exactly what I did.

Simon   Oh yeah, of course . . . Of course, and it's no coincidence is it that you stayed out so late, made me miss my son's birthday after efforts I made.

Marsha   Well, I'm sorry. It's not every day that you get to go with your son to the cinema. God knows, you've never done it, have you? I saw the opportunity to go, and I said yes.

Anthony *enters from the bathroom.*

Anthony (*to* **Marsha**)   Look there, I've finished.

Marsha   Let me have a closer look.

Anthony   There . . . (*He opens his mouth wide.*)

Marsha   . . . OK, mister, you've convinced me this time. (*She gives him a kiss on the cheek.*) OK, go on, say goodnight to your dad and go to sleep.

Anthony *walks up to* **Simon.**

Simon (*giving him a kiss and a hug*)   Sorry I missed your birthday, son, huh?

Anthony   It's all right, Dad.

Simon   See, your mother made a mistake. She stopped me from coming out with you,

Marsha   That's not true.

Simon   Because she'd prefer to bring someone around and take you out with them instead of me. (*Slight pause.*) And I bought a cake for you, and a present. I mean, look, it doesn't feel right if we don't at least blow the candles out on your cake, what d'you say? You wanna do that?

Marsha   Can't we do it in the morning?

Simon   I'm asking Anthony. What'd you say, son?

Anthony   But Dad, I just finished brushing my teeth.

Simon   Well, son, no one's asking you to eat the thing! . . . I bought you a cake, for God's sake! You just gotta blow out the candles, that's it. (*He laughs off his frustration.*) You gotta make a wish. If you don't make a wish that's your one chance gone, son. You gotta do it, you're a year away from being a teenager, that's something special.

Anthony *looks at* **Marsha** *for approval.*

Marsha   This is so ridiculous, Simon.

Simon *goes into the bedroom and retrieves the present.*

Simon (*on entering*)   And look here, just take a look at how much I love you, boy.

Anthony   Oh man, is that mine?

Simon   Son, it's yours and yours only . . . and if you'd have come home earlier, I could have given this to you. We could have listened to Gershwin together.

Anthony   It's Gershwin, Dad?

Simon   That's what I said, son. Gershwin and Rachmaninov and all the greatest things.

Marsha   OK there. You've done it, you've got a great big present for Anthony – there, you've done it!

Simon   Shut up, OK.

Marsha   Anthony, you can do all this in the morning.

Simon   Hey . . . I'm warning you!

Anthony   Dad, maybe I'll cut the cake in the morning?

Simon   You wanna cut the cake in the morning? OK, fine, forget the cake, OK? Instead, take a look at what I got you.

He places the present on the table. **Anthony** *doesn't respond.*

Simon   Come on, I know you're a bit tired, but you're young, you're supposed to have tons of energy!

Marsha   Simon, let him go to bed.

Anthony *gets up, feeling slightly uneasy.*

Simon (*making* **Anthony** *sit down*)   Now look here, look what I got right in front of you. (*Slight pause.*) Why don't you open it, boy?

Anthony *hesitates, conscious of his mother's objections.*

Simon   Come on, son, you gonna do what I asked you?

A tear rolls down **Anthony**'s *face. He wipes it away with his hand.*

Simon   What's . . . why you crying for?

Anthony   I'm not, Dad, I'm not crying.

Marsha   Leave him alone, please.

Simon   Come on then . . . do it for Dad. Don't be a wimp.
Come on . . . I'll help you. (*He pulls open the present.*) There, look.
Look at that. You like it?

Anthony   Yeah, Dad, it's great, I like it.

Simon   . . . Well, play something. Why don't you do that?
Come on, son. Show me you like it. (*Pause.*) I've been waiting
for ages to celebrate your birthday, and it means so much to
me, but instead your mother decides to take you out and have
you celebrate your birthday without me – you think that's fair?

A pause, **Anthony** *doesn't move.*

Simon   Now, you're my son, you'll do what I say.

He rips open the box: an electric keyboard is revealed.

Here, you go play something if you want.

Marsha   Now you leave him!

Simon   You happy? Turning my son against me? I love
my boy and he's happier about a flipping coin than what I
bought . . . (*Pause.*) Play. I love you, son. Do one, just do 'Misty'
for me? How about it? Your whole class have seen you but
I haven't yet.

Marsha   Simon, I'm warning you, you leave him be!
Anthony, go to bed! (*Reaching for him.*)

Simon (*turning to* **Marsha***, grabbing her*)   Listen here, I'll
fucking . . . say another word. (*To* **Anthony**.) Don't fucking
move, Anthony!

Anthony (*getting up*)   Let me do it tomorrow, please, Dad.

Simon   Sit down!

Anthony *sits back down. A pause.*

Simon   Look, there's no batteries. (*He unwraps the plug.*) Let
me just plug it in, look now.

Anthony *defiantly backs away from the keyboard.* **Simon** *grabs him by the arm and drags him to the keyboard.*

Simon   Come here . . . Now I'm you father. I bought this for you, now you play it! You show me some goddam appreciation!

Anthony   No, I don't want it! Get off me. I don't want it – I hate it!

In a show of anger he aggressively pushes the keyboard away from him. It accidentally falls off the table. In an instant fit of rage, **Simon** *grabs hold of* **Anthony** *and holds him head down onto the table.*

Marsha   Simon, no!

Simon   I gave birth to you!

There is a silence. **Anthony** *is trembling. In an instant, as if waking up,* **Simon** *realises what he is doing. He stares down at* **Anthony** *in disbelief. He lets go of him.* **Anthony** *jolts up off the table and runs out of the house.* **Marsha** *tries to hold on to him but he pushes her away and runs past her.* **Simon** *looks up, staggers and drops to his knees in shock.*

Simon   . . . I made a mistake . . . Tell him . . . I made . . . a mistake.

Halfway through his saying this, **Marsha** *bursts out of the house screaming* **Anthony**'s *name.*

Marsha   Anthony! . . . Anthony!

Lights down.

Act Three

Scene One

It is a few days later. **Simon** *is in the flat. Around him on the table are empty bottles of beer and cigarette packets. He smokes a cigarette. He sits hunched over, listening to Sergei Rachmaninov on the CD player. There is a healing quality in the music which he responds to. While doing this, he momentarily searches through a small pile of CDs, looking for the Gershwin. The house is in a worse mess than in the previous scene, and the keyboard is still on the floor. The front door is open.* **George** *is seated at the other end of the table.*

A silence.

George (*without looking at* **Simon**)   He's gonna be something when he grows up, huh?

Simon   He's gonna be a musician.

George   The amount of people's hearts he'd be breaking, women's hearts, with that face alone, forget the music. (*He laughs. Pause.*) It's lucky I brought you inside last night, if you'd stayed outside all night you would've been frozen over.

Simon   I couldn't stay inside.

George   You young are so health-conscious. In my day you wanted to forget about things, you had a drink and a smoke down the pub. (*Long pause.*) You got some things that other men in their lives could only wish for. I wish I'd been where you are in your place now . . . instead of turning my back on everything . . . and when you ain't got people in your life cos you're stubborn it eats you up. (*Pause.*) You should bring them back here.

Simon   I tried to phone, she didn't pick up.

George   That's not a reason to stop . . . Try again.

Simon   Maybe she don't want to see me.

Pause. **George** *gets up and puts his hand on* **Simon**'s *shoulder.*

George   Let the country fall apart around you, but don't let yourself fall apart.

Pause.

Simon   I'll go get them. (*He gets up.*)

George   Now that's a good idea.

Simon   She must've not heard the phone.

George   And also, Si, you know how much she wants to take me up on my offer – you could do the same.

Simon   I gotta do things myself, George.

George   Yes, I know that, but don't be too proud to take the help that's there. (*Pause.*) And the sooner you sort yourself out, the sooner you'll be able to get rid of that idiot friend of yours that came here knocking the house down.

Simon   When did he come?

George   This morning. Maybe you were sleeping, he knocked my door and I told him to bugger off but he waited outside your door looking through your letter box, things like that . . . He said he'll be back in an hour, and that was about eleven this morning.

Simon   Yeah, well, I'm not interested in working for the time being.

George   He looked pissed off all right.

Simon   It'll be all right . . . I'll sort it out.

The intercom buzzes. It does so again, long and sustained. He gets up and presses on the intercom.

Yes?

There's no response He glances over at **George**, *then presses the intercom entrance button.*

George   I suppose you all wanna talk . . .

Simon   It don't matter . . . You can stay.

Paul *enters, rapping on the door.*

Paul (*pleasantly*)   Hey! Hey, mister! Mister!

Simon   Paul, how's tricks?

Paul   I'm fine, I just figured something was wrong – ain't heard from you, so I came down, there might have been a tragedy, ain't that right, old man?

George   George.

Paul   Yeah, of course, whatever. (*To* **George**.) So you looking after him?

George   That's what I'm doing.

Paul   Terrible, terrible thing that's happened . . . Simon, I mean Marsha, I love her but she needs patience. (*Pause.*) So how long they been gone? Couple days? (*Pause.*) Simon? Old man?

Simon   His name's George!

Paul   I'm kidding, relax. (*Pause. He smiles.*) OK, OK, Mr George . . . Look, I won't hold you up any longer, I'll keep him company from here, he's family.

George   We're just going over the details over the new mortgage he has, you interrupted.

Paul   Oh, really? New mortgage?

Simon   I'll be making a commitment to something else.

Paul   Ah, that's great! Good news . . . But with what money? The money I gave you?

Simon   No, not for this, Paul.

Paul   Well, you know, you could've even come to me if you needed a new flat . . . (*Pause. Looks at his watch.*) Si, actually – look, I need to make tracks soon . . . Just spare me a few minutes.

George (*to* **Simon**)   I'll excuse you.

Simon   You don't have to.

George (*getting up*)   That's quite all right. I'll come back, whenever's best for you.

Paul (*as* **George** *walks past*)   You're such a nice man.

George   Cut the shit.

Paul (*surprised, to* **Simon**)   Would you look at that? (*He laughs.*)

George   Yes, I don't like you. Prick.

George *exits.* **Simon** *gets up and puts his coat on.* **Paul** *looks at him. Long silence.*

Paul   The old people around here hate me. You off somewhere?

Simon   To see Marsha. Gotta clear things up with her . . . Made a bit of a mess of things.

Paul   But you know you got commitments, right?

Simon   Well, I'm done with it all, Paul.

Paul   Oh, of course, yes . . . You're done with it all.

Simon   That's right.

Paul   But wait a minute – you came to me, didn't you? You saw an opportunity? I gave it to you. You got everything you wished, so what wrong?

Simon   It's wrong for me.

Paul   But Simon, come on, you remember what I said to you before, huh? What was it . . . When we were sitting in the pub the other day. (*He thinks.*) 'Let me, if not by birth, have lands by wit.' You remember that? . . . That *King Lear* bollocks I learnt in prison . . .

Simon   What about it?

Paul   Think about it. Intelligent men like us born with nothing need to hustle to get what we need . . . Men like us have no fear of illegal shit, do we? An intelligent man loves the black economy, believes in it, thrives off it. He makes it his wife, and fucks it every night. (*He laughs.*) And when he gets up in the morning and he looks in the mirror, he sees himself grow into a giant. And that's when the doors open for you. (*Pause.*) It's always been this way. It's the fat and greasy who inherit this country, not us. It's not us that the streets are named after, son. Men like us gotta die in the nastiest ways to stand a chance of being remembered . . . Have some shit building in the middle of nowhere named after you. (*Pause.*) Nothing's really there for you, you know that . . . Just look how you lost your job. First insulted by some old bitch, then sacked? You think if the law was on your side you would've stopped doing the thing you loved most?

Simon   Oh, quit the bullshit, Paul!

Paul   What bullshit? It's the truth?

Simon   I lost my job fair and square. I broke the law, Paul, that's why I lost my job, nothing else.

Paul   Like hell you did, don't lie to yourself.

Simon   I broke the law! And if you don't believe me, I'll tell you . . . You know why I lost my job? You know why I did? I had this woman, I used to drop her at Latimer Station all the time every morning, eleven o'clock, the same 295 route. Every day she'll be waiting at the bus stop, and I'd smile at her as she got on. (*Slight pause. Almost tearful.*) One day, on that bus something happened, like she was having an attack or something.

Paul   You're making this up.

Simon   Now you listen to me. I burst open my cabin door, and I rush over to her, but she don't wanna let me touch her, you know. She's about seventy and she's saying that she needs help but she don't want me. So I tell her I own the bus, I tell her that I got first aid, and she didn't even hear me, she just blurted out that I probably didn't even speak English . . . That I don't even speak English, that I was trying to steal her stuff. Before she even took the time to listen she insulted me. And I got so angry I flipped out. Some stupid old piece of nothing was trying to put me down and I flipped out. (*Slight pause.*) I got so mad that I picked her up and I kicked her out of my bus,

threw her handbag out on the road. Left her on the pavement,
I didn't care . . . And they sacked me for that. You know? They
sacked me, not cos I was just standing up for myself, but
because I was a dumb fuck, I didn't use my brain. Why waste
all that energy to make her see that I am significant? Why waste
the energy? (*Pause.*) But I understand it now . . . I can be what
I want in this judgemental, disgusting place. I know how to
survive it . . . I won't go for nothing out of my reach. I won't
try to be nothing than the lowest thing. I'll just live my life out
of the way, in this ghetto or that – there's nothing special
enough in this place for me to want to fight for anything. I just
got two people in this world that I would sweat to death for
and that's all I need. And you, and them millionaires and
billionaires, you fight amongst yourselves for things you can't
take to the grave with you. But for me, I'm happy to watch
those things burn.

Paul   All right, I understand that . . . fine.

Simon   I'm sorry, Paul.

Paul   All right, fine! Fine! . . . Just give me the money back.

Simon   I already spent the money, you know that.

Paul   But you owe me.

Simon   I'll pay you the money back, just give me a bit of
time.

Paul   Hey, come on, give you a bit of time? Driving the truck
is all you gotta do. One more job, why give you time? I'm not
asking much else, am I?

Simon   Paul, I gotta go and see them now . . .

Paul (*grabbing hold of* **Simon** *as he walks past*)   Si . . . don't
make me . . .

Simon   Now look, I gotta go see them.

Paul   You know, Si, leave this house right, without doing
the rest of the things that you've been paid to do is putting
my livelihood in danger. A lot of people need to eat, you
understand? Now you don't come with me, it puts me in a lot

of shit. And I don't need to be in it . . . I'll have to let them know where you live.

Simon   What'd you say? Why?

Paul   Because I ain't gonna take no flak for someone who can't keep their word.

Simon   You wouldn't fucking do that.

Paul   It's out of my hands.

Simon   Get out.

Paul   I'll let them know where you sleep, Si, and as much as I love them, where your wife sleeps, where your son sleeps.

Simon (*getting up to throw him out of the house; about to grab hold of him*)   You get the fuck out of –

Paul   You get off me!

Simon   Is this what it comes to? I'm trying to keep my fucking family together and you're gonna put a price on my head?

Long pause. **Paul** *pushes* **Simon** *off.*

Paul   Simon, I got people on my fucking head. And I don't give a fuck if you lose your fucking mind, you ain't at work, you ain't covering the money you've been paid . . . you're on your own.

Simon   How can you do this to me? . . . How? (*Pause.*) I'm not just some guy off the street. I'm trying to keep my family together. Paul, this is me, I'm a man, you don't just buy me and sell me. (*Grabbing hold of him.*) Now hold on a sec, Paul, I'll do anything else, man.

Paul   Get off me!

Simon *falls to his knees.*

Paul   Be a man, you live up to your word.

Paul *pushes* **Simon** *off him and exits.*

Slow fade.

Scene Two

The next day. It is early evening, the moon is yellow and beginning to rise slowly. The house is in a considerably better state than the previous scene.
Simon, *wearing his coat, is just finishing up the cleaning, on his knees sweeping up the last remaining bits of dust. The keyboard rests near the wall in its box, which has been taped back after being ripped open.*
Marsha *enters the house quietly. She watches him. He turns to her.*

Simon   I've put the keyboard in the corner for him.

Marsha   You can give it to him yourself, can't you?

Pause.

Simon (*standing up*)   You came in so suddenly, you could scare the skin off a cat.

Marsha   You'd only be frightened if you had something to fear.

Simon   I've got nothing to fear, apart from making sure I don't miss not doing the things I want.

Marsha   It's important to do what you want.

Simon   It is . . .

Marsha   It's also important to make some sacrifices.

Simon   Why sacrifice? Everything in this life is always about sacrifice.

Pause.

Marsha   I got your message . . . (*Pause.*) So I came to talk.

Simon   I left another message, I said I'd come see you in a couple days.

Marsha   Where are you going?

Simon   Nowhere, just gonna go out and see the boys.

Marsha   Where?

Simon   Across the road. (*Slight pause.*) I made friends with this cab driver, the guy from Sudan, probably one of the funniest guys I've ever met, you know? . . . So it's like his last day, he's leaving. Thought I'd throw in a quick goodbye drink before he leaves.

Marsha   You could have a drink after.

Simon   No, it's best before, get it out of the way . . . I'll see you later, tomorrow if you can, I'll come to Hammersmith.

Pause.

Marsha   I'm worried. I've got this feeling, Simon. You leave this house, I've got a feeling that something bad is gonna happen.

Simon   Now what would happen to me? . . . When I get back . . . (*He moves past her.*)

Marsha   I want to know his name. This guy you're going to see – what's his name?

Simon   I don't remember.

Marsha   You've been working with him, you must know his name.

Simon   It's escaped me.

Pause.

Marsha   If you leave this house . . . I can't take you back if you do this.

Simon   The only way to make it right is to do this.

Marsha *grabs hold of him.*

Marsha   I respect a strong man, a man that can fight the real battles in life, the ones where he can face the challenges within himself and win them.

Simon   I'm fighting my battles now . . .

Marsha   I just want the Simon I used to know.

Pause.

Simon   Let me go . . . I gotta go.

Marsha   Baby –

Simon   – A lot of money needs paying back.

Marsha   So get another job . . . If I have to, I'll work overtime . . . I'll pay. I don't mind. (*Slight pause.*) Where did it all go anyway?

Simon   The house.

They look around, then both laugh.

Marsha (*with tears in her eyes*)   But it looks the same. It's the same house.

Long pause.

Simon   The moon, it's come out so early, hasn't it? The sky, it's beautiful-looking, it's so nice to see the moon when it's so yellow.

Pause. He holds on to her.

I come back, we'll talk to George.

Marsha   As long as you make it back.

Simon   I will, in about seven hours.

Marsha (*after a pause; trying to be casual*)   Do you want me to wait for you or not?

Simon *tries to speak but can't.*

Marsha   I don't mind.

He lets go of her and walks to the door.

Marsha (*finding it hard to express her feelings; strained, she rubs her forehead*)   I love you . . . you know that. (*With a light-hearted smile.*) Even if it is only through habit.

Simon *stops. He half turns, not looking in her eyes.*

Marsha   You come back here, we'll do what you said . . . Go see George . . . (*Pause.*) And Anthony, Anthony loves you, you know that.

Simon *stops and turns.*

Marsha   He's afraid that you don't love him any more.

Simon   Oh that boy, I'll . . . (*As if about to lose his composure, he stops.*)

Marsha   Maybe he's just like his father, in many ways. His heart sometimes needs looking after.

Simon (*with tears in his eyes*)   Tell him that he's always gotta be better than his class, right? Always.

They share a brief smile.

Marsha   I'll wait here for you.

Simon *tries to say something, but can't. He exits.* **Marsha** *lets out a sigh. She walks to the door and takes off her coat and scarf. She walks back to the table. In an instant her heart seems to swell. She bursts into tears, she can't stop.*

Epilogue

The lights fade, but not completely to black; possibly a violet light bathes the stage. Simultaneously, a contemplative, sombre guitar rhythm plays. The lights gently rise again on **Marsha** *and* **Anthony** *entering the house. It is sometime in the near future. No words are spoken.* **Marsha** *takes off her own and* **Anthony***'s coats and instructs him to sit at the table.* **Anthony** *does so and takes out his school books.* **Marsha** *meanwhile prepares the cooking. She simultaneously juggles preparing to cook some rice and watching over* **Anthony***'s homework. This appears exhausting for her. She stops and looks at* **Anthony**, *lets out a sigh and runs her hand through* **Anthony***'s hair; however, this is promptly flicked away.* **Marsha** *rubs her forehead. The door opens and* **Simon** *enters. He is coming home from work. It is office work of some kind. He hugs* **Marsha** *and sits next to* **Anthony**, *who shows him his homework.* **Simon** *takes* **Anthony***'s exercise book, looks at it, then picks it up and taps* **Anthony***'s head with it, also producing a chocolate from his pocket, which* **Anthony** *grabs.* **Marsha**, *noticing this, walks over and takes the chocolate from* **Anthony**, *despite his mild protest. She replaces it with a plate. They begin setting the table.*

Slow fade.